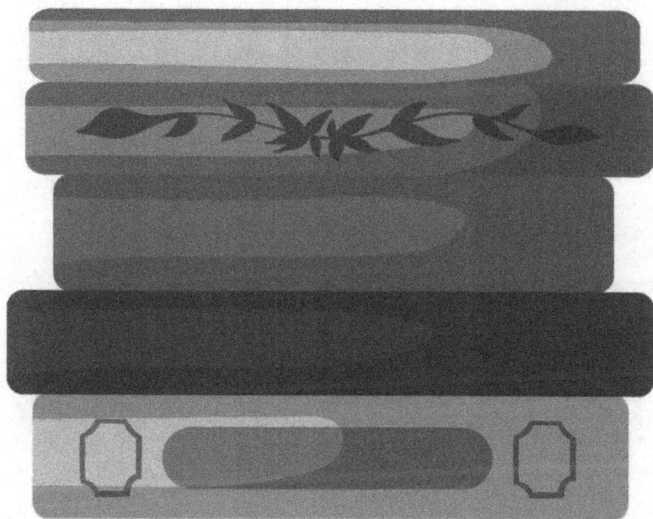

All
Booked
Up

A READING

RETROSPECTIVE

SUSAN ELKIN

The Book Guild Ltd

First published in Great Britain in 2024 by
The Book Guild Ltd
Unit E2 Airfield Business Park,
Harrison Road, Market Harborough,
Leicestershire. LE16 7UL
Tel: 0116 2792299
www.bookguild.co.uk
Email: info@bookguild.co.uk
Twitter: @bookguild

Typeset in 11pt Adobe Caslon Pro

Printed and bound by CPI Group (UK) Ltd, Croydon, CR0 4YY

ISBN 978 1916668 416

British Library Cataloguing in Publication Data.
A catalogue record for this book is available from the British Library.

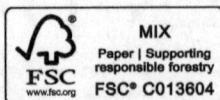

MIX
Paper | Supporting
responsible forestry
FSC® C013604

For Karen Burr, my daughter-out-law, who gave me the idea for this book.

1. CHILDHOOD

Five Go Off in a Caravan by Enid Blyton (1946)

I'm about seven. Aunty June and I are sitting in the big armchair in the room behind the shop – our cosy, crowded, cramped sitting room. It's pretty small by modern standards with what passes for a kitchen in a small alcove so there are cooking smells. Our dining table (we do a lot of squeezing past furniture or, in my case, wriggling under it) sits in front of doors out to the garden at the back. There is a door to the staircase between this back room and the shop too. That also leads to a cupboard under the stairs which my mother uses as a larder and where I am often sent to put a shilling in the gas meter. We have a fireplace and an open fire surrounded by a big brass fireguard to keep my one-year-old sister safe. My mother often airs bits of washing on the fireguard. Somehow my parents have also squeezed a sideboard – atop which sits my father's radiogram – and a green 1950's kitchen cabinet with a dropdown flap into that space which tends to be full of people. Family members, favoured shop customers who need to be plied with tea and various friends of all ages pass through continually.

But today it's just Aunty June and me. And she's reading to me from a book with a red cover. It's called *Five Go Off in a Caravan*. I don't know how it had been acquired. The chances are that it had 'come into the shop' like most books and other items in my childhood. The family business was officially 'antiques and Victoriana' and we lived behind and above The Corner Shop which occupied a big corner site at the junction of Blythe Vale and Stanstead Road between Forest Hill and Catford in South London. My father and his brother, Terry, who had a similar smaller shop in nearby Sydenham, were in business together. They bought antiques all the time (and I still have some of the things that they kept rather than selling on) but along with the pricey, saleable pieces often came useful everyday items so almost everything we used – from chairs, to electrical equipment to crockery – was second-hand. Things simply 'came into the shop'. There were always lots of books. Both my father and Terry had racks of second-hand books outside the shop for customers to browse through. Anything which looked remotely suitable was handed to me although my mother usually insisted on covering second-hand books with brown paper because we didn't know 'where they'd been'.

Aunty June was an enthusiastic reader. She was actually my father's first cousin lodging with my paternal grandparents down the road because her own parents lived in the country and she had taken a job at Lewisham Telephone Exchange. In time she met and married a south Londoner and they moved away. But for several years she was a key figure in my childhood – she taught me to knit, for example, and took me to lots of nice places including to stay with her parents, my great aunt and uncle, first in Somerset and later in Berkshire.

There was something about her reading *Five Go Off in a Caravan* which spurred me on because shortly after that I picked it up independently and read it right through to myself. My mother, who'd been an infants' teacher, had taught me to read before I started at Rathfern Road School round the corner at age five and three months. I therefore sped through the compulsory Beacon readers in the first few weeks at school and began to read age-appropriate books independently. *Five Go Off in a Caravan*, however, was the first full length novel I read. I suppose it's what today's children call a 'chapter book' although we didn't use that term then. For me it was a milestone – the first on a life-long reading journey.

Nearly seventy years later I ordered a new paperback copy, published in 2017, to remind myself what it was that grabbed me – and millions of other children in my generation – so forcibly. Well, for a start, the idea of four children being allowed to go off on holiday in sole charge of two caravans and two horses without adults seems like fantasy and of course it was, although slightly less so to a 1950's child than a 21st century one. We were, after all, allowed to go out with our friends to explore from quite a young age, unlike today's primary school children who are, it seems, minutely supervised and organised for every moment of the day. I used to go to the park, library, swimming pool, shops and so on, independently long before I left primary school.

Julian, Dick, George, Anne and Timmy have seen a circus nearby at the beginning of the holidays so they persuade Julian, Dick and Anne's parents to let them follow it to another area. It suits the grown-ups because they have to go away on a business trip. In real life, the parents and their children might – just might – have wanted to spend some time together given that the children have been away at boarding school all term. Enid Blyton (1997– 1968), according to various biographers and her younger daughter, Imogen, was not the best of parents herself so maybe this 'hands off' approach didn't seem odd to her. Nonetheless you can't help chuckling at the exuberant, naive absurdity of "I know what we'll do these hols! We'll hire a caravan and go off in it ourselves. Do lets! Oh, do let's!"

Of course there are baddies in the circus, predictably outwitted by the children. Nobby, the circus boy who becomes their friend, is an appealing character and Blyton was always good at child/animal relationships. Pongo the chimpanzee is a delight and, inevitably he saves the day when the children are in serious danger. I doubt that, age seven, I'd ever seen a chimpanzee except possibly on *Zoo Quest*, Desmond Morris's memorably educative TV series.

As a septuagenarian, 21st century reader, with decades of English teaching under my belt, I am now very aware of the language. No one in the 2020s would write 'It was a wide road, but not a busy one, for it was a country district' with that old fashioned use of 'for' as a conjunction. Expletives like 'blow!' and 'dash!' seem ludicrously quaint although I'm quite glad that these things haven't been updated by feverish modern editors obsessed with 'accessibility'.

Enid Blyton wrote over seven hundred books. She sat on her sofa and worked on a portable typewriter. She could, apparently, knock out ten thousand words in a day and a Famous Five book in a week. I was struck, not for the first time, re-reading *Five Go Off in a Caravan* how much better the books would have been if she'd taken just a little more time and trouble. She was hurriedly lazy about adjectives and verbs. Witness the repetition of, for example, 'mutinous' and 'guffaw'. And she writes '"Woof," said Timmy' so often that it's passed into the culture like a Shakespearean aphorism. In Chapter 14 she informs us that 'His [Julian's] heart began to beat'. I'm surprised that, even in 1946 and dealing with the JK Rowling of the day, no copy editor spotted that.

My modern copy has cover illustrations by Laura Ellen Anderson with spikey, thin-legged, round-eyed children in tee shirts and jeans – designed, obviously to grab today's young readers. I missed Eileen Soper (1905–1990) though, so I also sourced a good copy of the original red-covered hardback first published in 1946. Mine is the ninth impression dating from 1956. Soper's pencil drawings of Julian in his baggy shorts and Anne in her little feminine frocks will always be my visual image of the Famous Five.

Well, having read it back in 1954, I was suddenly a child ravenous for more. *Five Go Off in a Caravan* is the fifth in the series so the first thing was to duck back and read the first four from *Five on a Treasure Island* (1942) onward. They appeared on birthdays and under the Christmas tree. If I was lucky they came into the shop. Or you could lend and borrow with friends who might happen to have one that you didn't and vice versa. Libraries weren't as helpful as they could have been because there was prejudice against Blyton, perhaps because of her popularity, and some librarians refused to stock her books. I have especially happy memories of *Five Go to Smuggler's Top* which was the fourth in the series. The touch-and-go rescue by Uncle Quentin in pyjamas of Timmy caught in quicksand is unforgettable – along with Soper's illustration.

Titles were still appearing too. A new hardback Famous Five book cost seven shillings and sixpence (35p) so that was the usual amount kind relatives gave as a Book Token. I would then go to WH Smiths in Forest Hill alone on the bus and order the title I wanted, which had to be gleefully collected a few days later. Today's Amazon generation really don't know how easy they have it. Having got the book in my hand I was usually so excited that I'd then sit in the park and devour half of it rather than going straight home. When we were in what would now be called Year 4, I spotted one of the boys deep in a brand new copy of *Five Have Plenty of Fun* which was hot off the press. He'd probably just had a birthday. I persuaded him to lend it to me when he'd finished it: cue for much adulation. I hope I gave it back to him in good condition. The series finally ended in 1963 with *Five are Together Again*, the twenty-first title. But by then I was sixteen and had moved on.

Blyton wrote hundreds of books which weren't about the

Famous Five and I gobbled those greedily too. *The Wishing Chair* and *The Magic Faraway Tree* are gloriously imaginative and I found them laugh-aloud funny in places – especially Saucepan Man who was deaf and forever mishearing things. It wasn't very kind but primary school me found him hilarious. The 'Adventure' series, featuring Philip, Dinah, Lucy-Ann, Jack and Kiki the parrot were aimed slightly older and included some very memorable scenes. Like most children I was pretty scared by the suits of armour with eyes looking out of them in *The Castle of Adventure*. As I read, I learned a lot from Jack's passion for ornithology. At the other end of the spectrum Blyton was churning out Noddy books which I was continually told to read to my sister, six years younger. Then there were the Mary Mouse books which I had to read to the twins, a year younger than me, whose mother sometimes looked after me after school when my parents were busy with their business.

So did I read anything other than Blyton? Yes, although I disliked fantasy then and now. So the Narnia books which were gradually appearing and being raved about by some adults, didn't grab me at all. I read and liked *What Katy Did*, *Black Beauty* and some of Malcolm Saville's titles. When Aunty June took me to stay with her parents at Bray near Maidenhead in Berkshire (Uncle Will was resident verger at the parish church) I found books she'd read as a girl still in the bookcase. Thus I discovered the Sue Barton books by Helen Dore Boylston and the Bobbsey Twins by Laura Lee Hope and read them avidly, realising for the first time that things are done differently in America. Checking these facts now, I find that Laura Lee Hope was a pseudonym. The Bobbsey twins were the creation of a syndicate which kept them going until 1992.

By the mid-fifties TV was more or less ubiquitous. The Coronation in 1953 was the turning point. Many extended families (mine included) got together in front of a hired set to watch the new young Queen get her regalia and were so impressed that soon afterwards people started to get their own at home. There was just one channel, the BBC, until the arrival of ITV in 1955. And TV lent itself to the adaptation of classic novels – usually in the Sunday teatime slot for cosy, round-the-fire family consumption. I saw and enjoyed both *David Copperfield* and *Jane Eyre*. That was how I came to have read abridged versions of both before I left primary school. I also had a good go at the unabridged versions but I'm not sure I ever finished them at that tender age.

So one way and another the reading was fairly eclectic but underpinned by Blyton until Aunty June gave me *The School at the Chalet* by Eleanor M Brent-Dyer for my tenth birthday. This was a series of school stories set in the pre-war and later Austrian Tyrol. Aunty June had loved them to bits in her girlhood and thought that I would too. She was right. Over the next two or three years I read about the first fifteen titles but the series was longer than that and, in the end, I grew out of them. I recently re-read *The School at the Chalet* and was astonished at the quality of the writing. The vocabulary is uncompromising and the narrative thoughtfully paced. It's a far cry from Enid Blyton and I realise now that if this is what I was reading at age ten or eleven it's hardly surprising I grew into someone with a wide vocabulary able to express ideas in writing fluently – it was a long time before I realised that many contemporaries couldn't do this. I liked school stories, by the way. I'd read the Enid Blyton St Clare's and Malory Towers stories and the occasional Angela Brazzil.

The other bit of reading that I'm really glad came my way was my weekly comic. My father was totally opposed to publications like *The Beano* and *Dandy* and wouldn't have them in the house, which didn't stop us having a peak at other people's copies when he wasn't around, obviously. He was, however, willing to let me have *Girl*, a sister publication to Hulton Press's *The Eagle* which was for boys. So it was delivered every week with the grown-ups' daily papers. My dad regarded, and referred to, it as a magazine rather than a comic. Yes, there were serialised stories in cartoon form such as *Belle of the Ballet* but what I remember most clearly are the mini-biographies of famous women. It was courtesy of *Girl* that I first met Elizabeth Fry, Florence Nightingale, the Brontes, Mary Slessor, Gladys Aylward and many more, which added much to my fund of general knowledge. When I go these days to review a show at Upstairs at the Gatehouse in Highgate I walk past a house with a blue plaque. Mary Kingsley lived there. Who? She was a Victorian traveller and ethnologist and I first heard of her in *Girl*.

I was interviewed, just before my eleventh birthday, by headmistress Miss May Yardley for admission to Sydenham High School, the grammar school I later attended. She asked me what I liked to read. I told her about some of the above and then added, "And Enid Blyton of course."

She sniffed prissily and said, "You ought to have grown out of that by now."

How wrong she was. Enid Blyton taught me to read. The decoding, drummed into me by my mother and consolidated at school, is the easy bit. It was Blyton who turned me into a life-long deep end reader – someone who can open a book and climb in. There's a hot line between the Blyton (or any other authorial) brain and the Elkin (Hillyer back then) brain. We need no other interpreter or assistance. The words hop off the page and transform themselves effortlessly into stories, ideas and pictures in my imagination. I feel deeply sorry for those who can't do that – the laborious sub-vocalisers, painstakingly articulating every word in their head, effectively reading aloud to themselves. It makes reading such an effort that of course such unfortunates are often reluctant to bother. I saw it all the time in the students I taught and I still see it in many adults now.

Enid Blyton was not a nice woman. She treated her first husband shamefully and denied him access to their daughters. She became prima-donna-ish. She wrote in a saccharine tone to her young fans about idyllic life at Green Hedges, Beaconsfield,

Buckinghamshire with her daughters, Gillian and Imogen. The daughters were actually away at Benenden School in Kent much of the time. Their mother, who swept in occasionally for visits, based Malory Towers on the building. Imogen, her younger daughter, has publicly claimed that her mother was violent and that her childhood was pretty miserable.

As ever, in my view, we have to separate the creator from the creation or the artist from the art whatever form it is. Her books got millions of children reading, just as Roald Dahl and JK Rowling did for later generations. And that's the most important thing about her work. Amazingly her books remain pretty popular too, despite changing social habits rendering them more and more remote and implausible. I know several under-elevens who have read and enjoyed them recently. *Five Go Off in a Caravan* is seventy-six years old at the time of writing but if it's still engaging young readers, that makes it a thing of real merit.

2. TEENS

Rebecca by Daphne du Maurier (1938)

There was no concept of transitional 'young adult' fiction when I was growing up. Publishers, such as Puffin, labelled anything considered suitable for under-sixteens as 'children's' and beyond that you assumed it was adult. It meant that we greedy readers simply had to find our own way into the wider literary world.

Today's teenagers have it much easier because there is a wealth of wonderful writers producing novels for exactly this age group; from *Sold* by Sue Barrow, which happens to be the most recent one I've read at the time of writing, to anything by Anne Cassidy, John Boyne and many more. *Sold* is a horrifying thriller about people trafficking from Albania. Lots of writers – Michael Morpurgo, for example – write for various age groups. His *Private Peaceful*, which is about the execution of shell-shocked conscripts in the First World War, is a long way from *Born to Run* which is about the plight of greyhounds. There's an enormous range of choice today which we didn't have in the 1950s once we started to graduate from children's books.

We never, incidentally, 'shared' a book in class in all the years I was in primary school. Teachers simply read something aloud to us occasionally, usually at the end of the day. I remember, for example, one teacher serialising one of Enid Blyton's Secret Seven books for us. And there was a student teacher who mesmerised me with some of Kipling's *Just So Stories*. I don't, though, remember any teacher talking to us about reading or in any way encouraging us to read all the lovely books that were available and likely to appeal to under-elevens. Perhaps they just assumed we did it so it didn't have to be promoted or encouraged. Most of the kids I knew read compulsively, after all. And it was a punishable offence to be caught reading under the desk during, for instance, an arithmetic lesson.

In 1958 I progressed to secondary school. In my case that meant a place at Sydenham High School, funded by the London County Council under the old direct grant scheme. This was because, like all my friends, I had passed the eleven plus exam. I don't quite know what I was expecting from something called an 'English Lesson' but what I got was an abridged version of *The Odyssey* in the first term, a reduced *Pilgrim's Progress* in the second and *A Midsummer Night's Dream* in the third – all done in little chunks and pretty dull. We mostly sat at our desks and there was a lot of reading round the class, although I do remember pushing the desks back and acting out Odysseus and Circe (I had to be a pig). We made a rather jolly, collaborative frieze showing all the incidents on Pilgrim's journey for the classroom wall too.

Actually *The Odyssey* was quite a good idea although it could have been more inspiringly done. It taught us a lot of basic things about Greek mythology which informed many of the things we had to read and study later. I liked *A Midsummer Night's Dream* too. We acted out the Rustics' play in the school garden and performed it for our parallel class. I played Peter Quince and somehow managed to learn his quite long prologue. That surprises me now because I've never been any good at memorising anything. There was a trip to Open Air Theatre, Regents Park to see the play but, sadly, I was ill on the day and couldn't go. I have, for the record, made up for it since; I've long since lost count of the number of times I've seen the 'Dream' in the 'Park'.

What all this instilled in me, however, at an impressionable age, was that there are two sorts of books. There are the ones you 'do' in school and the real ones which colour and inform the rest of your life. In my mind they quickly fell into two completely separate compartments and somehow the private ones seemed much more significant than the school ones.

When I was thirteen my parents, whose antiques business was proving pretty successful, bought a spacious Victorian house in Vancouver Road. It was a five-minute walk from the shop. Although, by then, they had bought the shop next door to extend both the showroom area and living accommodation, we'd still been pretty cramped above the shop. The new house provided a lovely big bedroom for each of us: our parents, my sister, me and our maternal grandmother who was by then living with us. There was lots of space downstairs too.

When we children were taken to see the house we were soon to move into, we met Mrs Davies, the vendor. Her husband was retiring from his butcher's business over the road and they were downsizing – although I don't think we used that term in 1960. In what was to be my gorgeous attic bedroom, for the next nine years until I married, was a bookcase full of books. These had belonged to Diana Davies, their grown-up daughter. Mrs Davies showed them to us and asked if we'd like to have them when we moved in. We didn't need asking twice. It was like being given a chest of treasure.

Over the next year or two I worked through everything there which was roughly age-appropriate. Some were for younger children and my sister, who was then seven, has her own happy memories of what she found in that bookcase. My favourite from this time was *The Swish of the Curtain* by Pamela Brown and its sequels. Diana had evidently collected them all. It's the story of a group of young people – early teens – who find an old shed with blue doors, convert it into a theatre and put on shows. One of them plays the violin, which struck a chord (pun intended) with me because I'd been playing since I was seven. Another is very practical in stage management terms and one of the girls is a gifted actor. I was quite stage struck by all this as well as learning a lot about theatre and performance. Of course I'd never heard of RADA until one of Pamela Brown's characters went there to train. The Blue Door Theatre gang were avid readers of a publication called *The Stage*. I'd never heard of that either but inferred that it was a trade newspaper. Little did I know that a few decades later, I would be working for *The Stage*, for a long time, writing features, columns and reviews on a regular basis. I visited RADA several times.

It's a good example of how you never read a fiction book without learning things. Every novel has to have a background and a setting and there are bound to be things in there which are unfamiliar. Voracious readers tend to have ragbag minds full of the snippets they've hoovered up effortlessly. As I used to say to my students: people who read fiction know things. I said it so often that they probably quoted it jokingly as a tedious Elkin aphorism behind my back. If so, I hope they still are because it's true.

My mother was a reader and there were always books around the house – typically tucked face down on the arm of the sofa because she'd been called away. They were on her bedside too and sat in little piles in the kitchen until she got round to shoving them in the bookcase or disposing of them because she'd read them. She was keen on detective fiction and sci-fi, especially John Wyndham, among other things.

One day, soon after we moved, I idly picked up her half-read copy of Agatha Christie's *A Pocketful of Rye* which was lying on the kitchen table. I read the first page, then the second... and suddenly realised that I could read this as easily as I could any of the children's books I owned or borrowed from the library. Yet this was a grown-up book! It was quite a heady, pivotal moment in my adolescence. I then consumed most of Agatha Christie and quickly worked out the whodunnit formula – the culprit is always going to be the least likely person, the one who couldn't possibly have done it. From this point I gradually felt my way into adult fiction.

Our parents had never supervised our reading or taken much interest in it. They just assumed – rightly – that we did it. Neither of them would have dreamed of reading one of our children's books once we no longer needed reading to. My father, who preferred biography and non-fiction, regarded fiction as a waste of time so he certainly wasn't going to be holding literary discussions with me. In fact, I was often told off for reading too much along the lines of, "For goodness sake, Susan, put that book down and lay the table as you've been told," or "Susan, you shouldn't have your nose buried in a book. You should be looking out of the car window at the scenery." It's hard to imagine any thinking parent actually trying to stop a child reading, these days, but it was a different world in the 1950s.

My mother, though, had been reading fiction all her life and, once I reached the adult books stage, was good at throwing out suggestions. I remember vividly when she read John Christopher's *Death of Grass* in 1956 and how excited she was about it, for example. I was only nine then so she certainly didn't pass it on to me until much later. By the time I was fourteen or fifteen though she often mentioned books – I read and enjoyed the 'Gollantz' series by Naomi Jacobs at her suggestion, for instance. She identified with them because the protagonists were antique dealers and, as for me, I've always been a sucker for a family saga – the seeds having been sown, I suppose, by the family at the heart of the Chalet School books.

Her best ever recommendation was *Rebecca* by Daphne du Maurier. It was published before the war in 1938 and she had read it when it first came out. She was sixteen then – just about the age I was when she drew my attention to it. I borrowed it from the library – in the old yellow-covered Gollancz edition – and was utterly transfixed.

For anyone interested in opening lines, 'Last night I dreamt I went to Manderley again' has to be one of the top ten in the whole of fiction. It's so arresting that I defy anyone not to want to read on. Du Maurier's descriptive powers are remarkable too. How about the menace in this: '"I came here when the first Mrs de Winter was a bride," she said and her voice which had hitherto, as I said, been dull and toneless, was harsh now with unexpected animation, with life and meaning, and there was a spot of colour on the gaunt cheek-bones.' Elsewhere we hear about housekeeper Mrs Danvers's dark figure and white skull-like face. We know as soon as we meet her that nothing is as it seems. The tension and excitement lies in the gradual unravelling and revelation.

Of course it's a reworking of the *Jane Eyre* story: penniless girl falls in love with wealthy landed man; haunted by first wife; and then conflagration. I loved the way we never learn the name of the initially timid, later strong, second Mrs de Winter who narrates. And of course I was riveted by the twist in the plot. Nothing is remotely predictable. It's a deeply compelling book.

I've read it many times since then so I know what's coming but I still go cold when I get to: '"I'd forgotten," said Maxim, and his voice was now tired, without expression, "that when you shoot a person there was so much blood."' The trust and love that he and the narrator gradually build up is very moving.

I then scuttled back to the library and borrowed everything I could find by Daphne Du Maurier. I loved *My Cousin Rachel* because it has a mystery at its centre in the same way as *Rebecca* does. I enjoyed *Hungry Hill* and the *Loving Spirit* (both family sagas). I liked *The Scapegoat* too. Some of her historical novels are good: *The King's General* is set in the Civil War and *Mary Anne* is about one of the author's own ancestors who was mistress to the Duke of York in the early 19th century. Although they're very popular I liked *Jamaica Inn* and *Frenchman's Creek* less. I loved the short stories though, many of which are quite experimental. Who could ever forget *The Blue Lenses* about a woman who had surgery which left her able only to see the people around her as animals which revealed awful things about their personalities? Both *The Birds* and *Don't Look Now* acquired new fame thanks to pretty terrifying films by Hitchcock (1963) and Nicholas Roeg (1973) respectively.

Meanwhile at school nobody was talking to us much about our own reading although one English teacher did read us a startling story called *Royal Jelly* at the end of one term, when we were about fourteen. It was about a sickly child whose parents fed him royal jelly to strengthen him. The result was that he gradually changed into a bee. I remembered it but it was a very long time before I realised this was one of Roald Dahl's *Tales of the Unexpected* which were televised and became popular in the 1980s. The volume which included *Royal Jelly* was called *Kiss Kiss*, published in 1960 so I imagine that our teacher had just read them herself, liked them and decided to share this particular story with us. If only there'd been more of that in our lessons.

The only other book recommendation I remember at school came from the geography teacher who actually understood that you can glean knowledge from fiction. We were studying Australia as one of our A Level topics and she suggested we read the novels of Nevil Shute as an easy way of getting the feel of Australia. So I embarked on *Beyond the Black Stump* and several other titles. When my mother got wind of this she pointed me to a *A Town Like Alice* which was, and is, a wonderful read. I re-read it about ten years ago and found myself crying at exactly the same spot that got me when I was a teenager. That's some book if it can move you at sixty-something just as it did at sixteen.

I didn't do A Level English (of which more anon) but was obliged, because the school was pretty enlightened in many ways, to attend a weekly general English lesson in the sixth form. One day the teacher, who was younger than many of her colleagues and usually quite good fun, asked us what we were reading. My friend (with whom I'd shared it) and I told her about *Rebecca*.

Her response still astonishes me, sixty years later: "You shouldn't be wasting your time with books like that," she snapped. Reactions? Well for a start, even at the time, I knew she was wrong. Nothing which had given me such enormous pleasure at every level could possibly be justifiably dismissed like that. Second, it was an insult too, although she probably didn't realise that. *Rebecca* had been lovingly recommended to me by my mother and there's something rather special about books shared between mothers and daughters. Third, it's actually quite rude to condemn something which someone else likes in that way.

It changed me though. I taught secondary school English for thirty-six years until I finally moved into full-time journalism and authorship. I told every class I ever taught about *Rebecca* and that teacher. I did it when I first met the students and promised them that they could and should talk to me about reading as much as they liked and that I would never, ever rubbish their choices. And I kept that promise faithfully. All reading is valuable. Moreover, it's only by reading eclectically that you learn to make informed choices and we all read at different levels at different times anyway. Another of my oft repeated comments was, "How are you going to learn to read critically if you don't read widely? You're not going to take my word for it about what's good and what's bad – or at least I hope you're not."

It meant that the students would often talk to me about books I hadn't read and I tried to heed their recommendations so it became a two-way process. My worst experience was *Flowers in the Attic* by VC Andrews (1979) which every teenage girl in the school was crazy about in the early 1980s. So I read it and detested the manipulative prurience relating to the levels of cruelty. But it meant I could discuss it with the students and explain why I hadn't enjoyed it.

Anyway, back to *Rebecca*. In 2004, when I was writing my English textbook series *So You Really Want to Learn English?* I opened one of the units with an extract from *Rebecca*: the creepy description of Rebecca's bedroom in Chapter 7. Soon after, I visited a prep school which was, gratifyingly, using my book. One of the teachers told me that her class (mostly twelve/thirteen year olds) had been so taken with the extract that they had pestered her into buying a complete set of *Rebecca* so that they could read the rest of the novel together in class. One in the eye for my own English teacher back in 1964, I thought, spitefully.

For the record, *Rebecca* has sometimes been set for A Level in recent years – often as a comparative text alongside *Jane Eyre*. Anyone who thinks this is dumbing down really needs to get out more and read a few more books.

I still have some of my old school reports which I found among my father's things when he died. When I was in the sixth form my form teacher wrote in her summary: 'Susan would write better essays if she read more'. As someone who has devoted her whole life to words in one form or another, and who has been eagerly devouring books since she was five years old, I laughed long and loud. I can only think (charitably) that she was having to write her reports late at night and that she was confusing me with someone else.

3. TEACHER TRAINING

The Light and the Dark by CP Snow (1947)

There is a photograph of me, not quite three, in my grandparents' garden. I am crouched in front of a miniature blackboard and easel on which someone has written a little sum. My lined-up dolls are listening to me as I tell them what's what. The date on the board is February 1950

I always said I was going to be a teacher, although before I went to school I can't really have had much understanding of what that meant. We were living with my paternal grandparents at that point – before my parents acquired The Corner Shop and independent living accommodation just along the road in 1952.

My grandfather was a teacher at the primary school round the corner where I would soon be a pupil. My father taught maths in a secondary school and my mother was an unqualified supply teacher. They all went off to work each morning leaving me with my grandmother and, I suppose, from all this, I imbibed a sense that grown-ups became teachers so that's what I would do too.

I stuck to my guns. Fast forward fourteen years and I needed to think about training. There were two options. University graduates were regarded as qualified teachers. They could simply go into secondary schools and teach their subject. The Post Graduate Certificate in Education (PGCE) already existed but it wasn't a requirement as it is today. The alternative was non-graduate vocational training at a teacher training college – which is what my grandfather and father had both done as part of post-war initiatives to get men returning from the war into civilian jobs, the former in 1920 and the latter in 1948.

No one at school ever suggested that I might be university material. And I was happy enough with that having drifted through school as a mediocre but adequate achiever who loathed science and maths. I also had – and have – a serious problem with rote learning and any form of committing to memory. It's a good job I had no ambition to be an actor.

No one recognised my problem (if that's what it was) at the time and it took me a very long time to work it out for myself. Howard Gardner famously identified seven styles of learning and types of intelligence. I don't think I fit any of them. As always, categorisation and labels can be very reductive. My learning style seems to require narrative. Thus, I'm dreadful with numbers. Maths is, for me, a sea of incomprehensible abstractions. On the other hand, I'm good at dates because if I think of 1815 the whole story of Waterloo starts to roll in my head. Mention 1649 and I can see Charles I on the scaffold outside a first-floor window at the Banqueting House in Whitehall. 1934 was the year Edward Elgar died so I can 'hear' the cello concerto and visualise Sir Edward striding around the Malvern Hills in his tweeds. It's all about stories and once I've contextualised something I'm on top of it. Unfortunately most of the exams I did at school relied on a very different sort of learning so my teenage achievements were unremarkable.

In 1965, the minimum qualification for teacher training college was five O Levels, subjects immaterial. It was an alarmingly low bar, looking back, and probably accounts for some of the woefully poor standards of teaching in many schools in the 1970s and 80s.

Well, I had six modest passes at sixteen, and soon added more, including the tiresome maths which I just about managed to scrape though on a second attempt. So what was I going to do in my last two sixth form years? I had been fascinated by biology from the very beginning of secondary school so, although I really am no scientist, here was an opportunity to immerse myself in it and it didn't matter how well (or not) I did in the subject. I'd been longing to do A Level zoology for years, and to its credit, the school allowed me to do it, alongside the serious scientists who were heading for medical school and the like. The only subject the timetable could fit in with it, as I wasn't up for the standard physics, chemistry and zoology package, was geography so I did that along with an additional O Level in human biology. And I can honestly say I loved it all – I was in those lessons for the love of learning and there can be no better reason for studying anything. The fact that I didn't excel at any of it didn't matter at all.

Meanwhile a friend, Peter, from church, three years older than me, had gone to Bishop Otter College, Chichester to train as a teacher. Along with other friends, I visited him there several times. Peter was evidently thriving and learning. It seemed a pleasant environment and knowing nothing about teacher training colleges I thought, *Yes, this would do nicely*. My parents reckoned it was a good idea too because a close family friend they respected had, by chance, trained at Bishop Otter fifteen years earlier when it was still an all-female establishment.

School was a stumbling block. You had to choose six colleges in order of preference. The headmistress, Miss May Yardley, told me firmly that I must not put Bishop Otter at the top of my list because it was, she explained loftily, a highly sought after college which required good A Levels. Instead she recommended that I apply for St Osyth's, Clacton. That was an all-female college which sounded hideously frumpy and old fashioned. Later I met someone who was training there who confirmed that it was just that. I knew Peter had just one A Level and a handful of O Levels so I asked him to do a quick survey of his college friends. When he sent his findings it transpired that few of them had anything approaching three high grade A Levels so I ignored the school and applied. I put St Osyth's at the bottom of my list and told my parents firmly that I was definitely not going there. "If it comes down to that I shall do something else," I said.

In the event, I got into Bishop Otter after an interview on the day the Conservative government finally fell in 1964. A week or two later, my mother opened the letter (by pre-arrangement) and phoned the school with the good news, asking the head to give me a message. Miss Yardley did have the grace to say, "Well done, Susan. I'm delighted for you," without further comment.

Then something rather wonderful happened. Bishop Otter sent me a reading list. It was long, eclectic and included lots of authors I either hadn't heard of or whose names I had vaguely been aware of but hadn't read. The list – and how I wish I still had it – was intended, I suppose, to get us teachers of the future better read than most of us probably were. Obviously, there was nothing compulsory about it. It was just a list of suggestions and maybe born of an assumption (accurate in my case) that we wouldn't have had much encouragement with wider reading at school.

And that was how I discovered CP Snow. I borrowed many of the books on that list from Lewisham Library and devoured them but for some reason I bought *The Light and the Dark* (1947) in paperback and I still have that, now very battered, copy. It was a unlike anything I'd read before. What did I know about life in Cambridge Colleges or 'manic depression' which we now call bi-polar? Nothing. That's one of the many strengths of fiction. There is no such thing as a novel from which the reader doesn't also gain factual, cultural or general knowledge however random it may be. That's why it's always useful to have a compulsive reader in a quiz team.

Snow's narrator, Lewis Eliot, is teaching in a fictional Cambridge College (it's Christ Church, where Snow was a Fellow, in all but name) during World War Two. His friend, Roy Calvert, glitters with brilliance and charisma. He's academically very talented, good company and attractive to women but beset by inner turmoil. Roy is, apparently, modelled on Charles Allbery, Snow's friend who was an Egyptologist. When I re-read it now, I still marvel at the way Snow presents a character who is, at heart, unfathomable, from the point of view of a man who cares deeply and does everything he can to help but, not being bi-polar himself, remains mystified and on the outside.

The Light and the Dark is the fourth novel in Snow's *Strangers and Brothers* sequence so of course I then doubled back and read the preceding three. I was always slightly puzzled by the first novel *Strangers and Brothers*. It's about the disgrace of a man named George Passant but Snow's prose is so subtle in places that I could never fathom exactly what Passant was meant to have done – something sexual, I suppose, and it's bound up with social class and snobbery. Or perhaps he'd done nothing and that was the point. The novel was later renamed *George Passant* because the original title was used to denote the whole series.

Snow (1905–1980) was still alive and producing novels when I discovered him. *Corridors of Power* (1964) was hot off the press and I worked forward towards it. *The Masters* (1951), which is about the selection of a new Master for the college, remains one of the most perceptive and telling studies of group dynamics and tribal loyalty – or lack of it – I have ever read. I think of it every time I'm involved with the election of anyone for anything at any level. I enjoyed and learned a huge amount from *The New Men* (1954) too. It examines the ethics of the development of nuclear weapons but relocating the research to Britain and involving some of Snow's ongoing characters.

The last two books in the series of eleven titles, *The Sleep of Reason* (1968) and *Last Things* (1970), were published after I left college. I bought them immediately in hardback although I think the earlier ones were probably better. Nonetheless there's an unforgettable account of the narrator's eye surgery in *Last Things*, which must have been written from experience, and taught me a lot, as fiction unfailingly does. Lewis Eliot narrates the entire series. Other characters flit in and out tangentially.

The whole sequence was adapted as a thirteen-part TV series for BBC by Julian Bond in 1984. I didn't much like most of it. Shaughan Seymour's Lewis Eliot was too cold and of course it lost the sense of a first-person narrative which is a key part of the novels. Nigel Havers, however, was perfect as Roy Calvert – one of those rare casting decisions when a character you've imagined through reading pops up on screen precisely as you'd envisioned him.

So one way and another, that reading list was a game changer with names like George Orwell, Graham Green, William Golding, Doris Lessing and lots more beckoning me. Arrival at Bishop Otter College in late September 1965, however, was not what I expected or wanted. Yes, it was great to have what felt like independence – a room in an onsite accommodation block (all funded by the state in those days), freedom to smoke almost anywhere if you wanted to, a kitchen to make drinks and light meals, the right to walk on and off site at will and so on. I can see now that it was really just like a liberal boarding school with a lot of rules. For example, the Principal had a thing about 'slacks' which we women were not allowed to wear in the dining room or supposed to wear in town. But it was a lot freer than my grammar school so at one level I was pretty happy. The buildings were nice too and, of course, Chichester was, and is, a beautiful city with a theatre which was then only two years old. We could buy tickets for five shillings (the whole of the back row was available at this price on the day) so we did and saw every show.

The curriculum, however, was a travesty. In 1968 Bishop Otter had, in its wisdom, jettisoned its former structured practice in favour of something 'holistic', trendy and totally different from the experience of my friend Peter who had left the year before and was now back in South London in his first teaching job. It seems unimaginable today that such a drastic change had been made without informing the incoming students but the system was dogged by top-down decision making in 1965.

We spent the whole of the first week building up to a strange dance drama about evolution involving every first year student writhing on the hall floor. Before that we had disjointed days in which pairs of staff from different departments did woolly things with groups of students. I have wiped most of the detail from my mind because I hated it and was bored out of my mind by most of it.

In the second week we started the curriculum proper in which we were divided into four groups. There were four themes and each group worked their way through them during the year. One was 'the nature of man'. The others were equally vague as staff members floated in and out. I remember several whole mornings playing (literally – we weren't allowed to relate them to numbers) with Cuisenaire Rods while the head of maths grunted over us. Then there was a session on bookbinding with the art department along with lots of strange antics wearing PE kit.

Trainee teachers were supposed to have a main subject that they specialised in. Peter had done science as his main subject for three years at Bishop Otter College. One of my school friends, an exact contemporary, was doing English at Stockwell College Bromley. But I was bouncing from one disparate, apparently irrelevant activity to another – never sure what I was supposed to be doing from one day to the next and disconcerted by the incoherence of it all. If we had an assignment to do the instructions were never incisive so that was off-putting too. Being asked to pen something was a relief, though, because I've always been able to write as long as I know what I'm meant to be writing about. On one occasion I called on one of the lecturers in her study and told her I simply didn't understand the assignment so could she explain it again, please. Her reply: "You worry too much, Miss Hillyer," and I got no further elucidation. Is it any wonder I got fed up?

I remember being told – over one holiday – to make a book on any subject I liked. So somehow I, who have very little arts and crafts expertise, was supposed to produce something imaginative, original and creative which looked good. How was that supposed to make me a better teacher? I did it – sort of – with help from a friend who can draw and using a simple loose-leaf format. Unsurprisingly it didn't get much of a mark although I don't actually know what the mark was because Bishop Otter had a peculiar new policy of never revealing to the student the mark awarded for anything. Staff knew our marks but we didn't. We had to make do with comments. No, the 1960s were not education's finest moment.

Another unusual Bishop Otter policy was that when you, at last, came to your main subject in the second year you could choose anything you liked. No previous knowledge or experience was required. I'm not sure that it was an educationally sound idea but it was what saved me and proved to be one of the biggest turning points in my life. There weren't that many subjects to choose from. I didn't want to do any more geography and I'd taken biology to the limits of my capabilities. Had there been a music option I might have done that. I had Grade 8 violin under my belt by then but it was only a scrape pass and I don't think I'd have been much of a music teacher.

In the event I chose English. I'd always been a reader as this book makes clear but I hadn't done A Level and had found O Level English literature pretty pedestrian. Was this the opportunity to discover it properly?

The English department at Bishop Otter was outstanding –
it was everything the college in general wasn't. Run like a small
university department it divided us into small groups (nine in the
group I was in) and assigned us a tutor whom we met each week
in his study for practical criticism. My tutor was Paul Townsend
and he was a fine teacher. He coaxed, demonstrated, facilitated and
encouraged us. Every session was full of learning and I could feel
myself growing as we studied the source material for *Antony and
Cleopatra* one week and a Larkin poem or a passage from Austen
the next. He even invited us to his home in Peterborough, where
Alec Guinness was a neighbour, for supper with his wife at the
end of term. Suddenly I knew that, at last, I really was in the right
place.

At the same time we were studying Shakespeare (of which more
in the next chapter) and via a complex series of options finding our
way into the delights of George Eliot, Thomas Hardy, Jane Austen,
Dickens, Trollope, Wordsworth, John Donne, Chaucer and a lot
more. It was refreshingly grown up too. We were expected to read
the texts independently and come to sessions able to discuss them.
And we were required to write proper essays at last so that was a
relief after the wasted first year. It was a wonderful time.

By then, in our second year, we were billeted out in digs in the
city so I couldn't go back to my room in the gaps during the day.
Instead I spent every available minute in the library making up for
lost time and acquainting myself with every critic and commentary
I could lay hands on – educating myself in this fabulous subject as
fast as I could. I wonder if I was the only student in my year to read
and make notes on nearly all of G Wilson Knight's classic books
about Shakespeare for example? No one, not even Mr Townsend,
directed me to do this, by the way. I was on a self-propelled mission.

Sadly (should I really have been at university?) English was
only half the story. The other half of the curriculum was Education.
There were very dull lectures about various education reports and

much talk about the Newsom Report of 1963 and the Plowden Report which was published in 1967. They also told us how to organise the furniture in a classroom, set up a nature table and to be 'child centred' most of which seemed irrelevant to me. Although my course was labelled Junior/Secondary I had decided that I was interested only in secondary. I was going to be a secondary school English teacher although there was absolutely no help in how I might teach this lovely subject I had so recently discovered to pupils in the future.

Never did anyone mention diversity either. Special needs were dealt with in a single visit to a residential institution which looked after comedian Bob Monkhouse's son, Gary, who had cerebral palsy and died in 1992 aged forty. We were casually told to read Stanley Sergal's book *No Child is Ineducable* (1967) which argued that every child should have education rights and led to the change in the law in the early 1970s. Before that, someone like Gary – who would have been about fifteen when I encountered him – could simply be deemed 'ineducable' and denied any form of schooling.

No one talked about discipline or behaviour management either. And, for someone aiming to teach in a secondary school there should, surely, have been training in exam teaching, especially the new CSE courses which were introduced in 1965 as a watered down, accessible alternative to O Level. Or what about running a form/tutor group? Basic first aid would have been jolly useful too. There were more holes in my teacher training than in a colander.

In my spare time – in bed at night or on the train for visits home, for example – I was still working through the reading list which I'd now been referring to for over two years and that included CP Snow with whom I was soon up to date.

In our third year we had to produce a 'special study' on a subject of our choice. No doubt these days it would be glorified as a 'dissertation' but we weren't a university so it wasn't. There used to be much more precision about these distinctions. I chose to write mine on the presentation of women in the *Strangers and Brothers* sequence. On the whole, Lewis Eliot as narrator describes and moves in a male-dominated world, as Snow investigates power in all its forms, but there are wives, girlfriends, sisters and so on and I was interested in how these function in the novels and what their role is. I concluded that they are actually indispensable, having examined each of the main ones minutely and re-read each of the books, in most cases for the third time.

The family friend who'd once trained at Bishop Otter got one of her office practice students to type it up for me as an exercise. I submitted it and emerged from Bishop Otter with a merit in English which really pleased me because it was the sort of achievement I'd never managed at school. I'd pretty much taken up the subject from scratch. And I'd done it despite the distraction of falling in love with my future husband, another friend from home, in my third year.

During the summer holiday immediately after I left Bishop Otter, Nick, my fiancé, and I went on a canal boat holiday in Shropshire with another couple, both old friends. I can remember sitting on the deck in the sunshine reading *The Last Chronicle of Barset* by Anthony Trollope with whom, incidentally, CP Snow is sometimes compared. We'd done some work on *The Warden* and *Barchester Towers*, both completely new to me, at college and I loved them. So I'd been happily working my way through the remaining four novels in the 'Barsetshire' series – and had now reached the finale. Yes, reading is like hopping across an infinite and complex series of stepping stones. And Bishop Otter College, for all its faults, started me off in many directions.

4. SHAKESPEARE

Macbeth by William Shakespeare (1606/7)

The unit on tragic drama was by far and away the best thing I experienced in three years at Bishop Otter College. It was such a catalyst that it – and everything that has flowed from it ever since – gets a chapter on its own here.

It was taught by head of the English department, Miss Marjorie Hiller. There were no fireworks or gimmicks. She just told us what texts to buy and read, and then sat behind her desk at the front and talked about them. And she was riveting. We began with *Macbeth*.

Now I think I'd read *Macbeth* in a desultory way at school in the pre-O Level years along with *A Midsummer Night's Dream*, *Twelfth Night*, *The Merchant of Venice* and *Julius Caesar*. It certainly wasn't completely new to me although no one had ever brought the text off the page making it fizz with nuance and subtext in the way Miss Hiller did, as she spoke and we made marginal notes.

I still have the Arden copy I used then – with her notes and sometimes irreverent comments. When Macbeth says, 'But the Thane of Cawdor lives', she pointed out, for example, that he was playing 'very dumb' because he must have known what had happened on the battlefield. When Lady Macbeth says, 'From this time/I account thy love', my perceptive note from Miss Hiller reads, 'She would not invoke their love unless it was a substantial thing'.

No one had ever brought Shakespeare to life like this for me before and I fell permanently in love in the first hour. It was the immediacy of the drama and the humanity of the words which suddenly fell movingly into place and captivated me. These creations were flesh and blood people the like of whom (in some form) I knew in real life. They weren't boring cardboard cut-outs from the past invented for the torture of 20th and 21st century students and audiences.

I was very happily married for over fifty years until Nick died in 2019 (of which more later) but Mr Shakespeare has always been my other man. And our 'affair' definitely dates from that classroom at Bishop Otter College in the autumn term of 1966.

After a few weeks we moved on to *King Lear* and another series of breathtaking revelations. Moreover, Miss Hiller told us to study independently at least one other Shakespeare tragedy so I immersed myself in *Anthony and Cleopatra* largely because it was the text my friend back at school had done for A Level so I'd heard a bit about it. It was like a series of doors opening ever wider.

That bit of the course was studying 'tragedy', not just Shakespeare, so it was also my introduction to both Ibsen and Chekhov. I knew of *Peer Gynt* because I was musical and, obviously, familiar with Grieg's famous incidental music but otherwise this was two more huge *oeuvres* completely new to me. The old Una Ellis-Fermor translations of Ibsen, which were all we had, seem a bit stilted now that so many other people have translated the plays in a more relaxed way, but I was drawn in nonetheless. At the end of term we went, *en masse*, to the Nuffield Theatre in Southampton to see a production of *Ghosts*.

We also had a look at the Theban Plays by Sophocles. I had actually seen a production of *Antigone* at a local school back home because someone I vaguely knew (friend of a friend) was in it, so we cluttered off there in a group to support her. It was, at least, an introduction to a group of plays which I have, of course, seen many times since in all sorts of formats and translations.

Obviously there were assignments and we had to see Miss Hiller, individually, to be given them back. We never, incidentally, called her anything else and I had to do quite a bit of Googling to dig out her given name for this book. She liked my *Macbeth* essay and commented in the margin: 'You have a good vocabulary'. Well yes – I suppose it was down to all the books I had read before I was nineteen. She told me my essay on servants in Ibsen was excellent and talked about it quite excitedly for several minutes. Of course I don't know what the mark or grade was but eighteen months later, when I was compiling my portfolio of coursework for final assessment, Mr Townsend consulted his mark book, peered over his glasses and said: "You MUST include that Ibsen essay."

For the rest of my time at Bishop Otter I opted for every course or unit on Shakespeare, thus encountering for the first time plays such as *As You Like It* and *Much Ado About Nothing* but none of the other staff or approaches came close to the magic of Miss Hiller's classes.

At the beginning of the third year, just before term started, there was a compulsory Stratford trip. We were required to get ourselves there and arrange our own accommodation – yes, we'd left school and were supposed to be grown up and it was fine but I doubt that any teacher would ask students of that age to do this now. Miss Hiller and some of the other staff met us before the shows and there were enlightening debriefings. We saw *Romeo and Juliet* with Ian Holm as Romeo and Estelle Kohler as Juliet, which was quite something and, looking back at the cast list now, I'm amused to note that Helen Mirren, who'd have been twenty-two, was on stage in an 'unnamed part'. The next day it was *Coriolanus*, directed by John Barton. Ian Richardson played the title role and

Mirren, who must have been part of that year's ensemble, was again in an unnamed role.

My passion for Shakespeare nearly didn't happen. No one in my family was interested at all, although I remember a special trip with my father when I was seven. He had to go to Coventry (no, I've no idea how that came about) to pick up some antiques in his van. It must have been school holiday time because I went too. This was probably to get me out of my mother's way because she would have had my baby sister to look after and a shop to run. It gave me a whole day with my father, just the two of us, which was very unusual and rather lovely, which is why I remember it so clearly.

We left early in the morning and ate a splendid hotel breakfast somewhere en route. At one point he needed to stop for a power nap. Unusually, I didn't have a book with me and the newsagent he stopped at didn't have a comic he was prepared to buy for me. So he bought me a tabloid newspaper. While he was asleep I read it from end to end. When he woke up I said: "Daddy, I've read all of this. Why do you call it the gutter press and say rude things about it? I enjoyed it."

He replied: "That's the whole point. You're only seven and it's meant to be for grown-ups."

On the way back from Coventry my father – who'd never seen a Shakespeare play in his life and never would – took me to Stratford and took a photograph of me, all summer dress, plaits and smiles, outside the Birthplace in Henley Street. I suppose he thought it would be good for my education – pretty prescient as things eventually turned out.

Otherwise my only experience of Shakespeare was secondary school where it was all done pretty dully. Nothing ever sparked my imagination or set me thinking about the real issues. And two years of exposure to *Henry V* for O Level came within a hair's breadth of killing Shakespeare for ever, for me. The teacher simply had no idea how to make it sparkle.

So how did Mr Shakespeare and I continue our relationship after I left college? Pretty quietly for a few years, although I did drive back to Chichester in 1969 to see Margaret Leighton as Cleopatra to John Clements' Antony directed by Peter Dews. The challenging Deptford boys' school I was ill-preparedly teaching in didn't seem to have heard of Shakespeare and it took every ounce of my energy and ingenuity just to keep my head above water. I did a bit of private coaching on the side, though, because we were living in rented accommodation and saving for a house. I helped one boy to pass his first O Level, English Literature, which included *Romeo and Juliet* and that was the first Shakespeare I ever taught. Then we moved to Wellingborough because of Nick's job and I was classroom teacher for a few years in a residential school for children with acute disabilities where no one would have dreamed of doing Shakespeare at that time. I like to think they might now.

The pivotal point came in 1977 when we moved to Kent and I went to work in an all girls' high school in Sittingbourne. A strange hybrid, it was fully comprehensive for the first two years. Then, aged thirteen, the most able students transferred to one of the local grammar schools, which Kent had retained and still does, leaving us with the traditional 'secondary modern' students, many of whom turned out to be late developers and did pretty well. There was another opportunity for grammar school transfer at sixteen.

In the English stock cupboard I found a tattily unloved set of *A Midsummer Night's Dream*, thought about it for a day or two and then asked the head of department whether she'd mind me using it with what we now call Year 7. "With these girls?" she said, astonished. "Well of course you're welcome to have a go but it's not likely to work."

So I dusted them off and embarked on my first ever attempt to take Shakespeare to the ordinary folk he meant it for. This would have been around 1978. There was no National Curriculum. Every school, every department and every individual teacher could do more or less what they chose – which is why so many students missed out on so much although, of course, there were others who got a rich mix. It simply depended on where you were and who your teachers were. In practice, though, the vast majority of students who weren't in independent or grammar schools went right through school without ever reading or hearing a word of Shakespeare. And some of the earliest pieces of journalism I did were columns saying just how wrong I thought this was. Yes, Shakespeare was always set for O Level and we did have a small O Level group in that high school, which eventually I taught. It's obviously, however, going to be far more difficult to make sense of, say, *The Merchant of Venice*, if you've never read any of that sort of language before.

My first stab at *A Midsummer Night's Dream* was not a runaway success but it certainly wasn't a failure. I got them to make a wall frieze and at the end of term I organised a trip to Regent's Park Open Air Theatre to see a production which was an exciting adventure for children from Kent, some of whom had rarely, if ever, been to London before although it was only 40 miles away. I was encouraged enough to do it again the following year with the next Year 7 and each time I did it, it went better. The students and I were learning together and that's always a big plus in education.

I'd started something too. After a year or two, I noticed that some of my colleagues were doing similar things. Soon I felt empowered to have a go at different plays with the equivalent of Year 8 and 9. There were three different heads of English over the eight years I worked in that school and gradually we acquired better copies of the mainstream plays. The ones published in the 'Oxford School Shakespeare' series edited by Roma Gill were modern looking and attractive with clear, helpful notes.

Then, Mr Shakespeare obligingly got me another job. We'd had a new headmistress who found the English department awkward, and, she (wrongly) suspected, subversive and threatening. So she called in the English local authority adviser/inspector to report on us to her. Trouble was, from her point of view, that we knew him better than she did. She was a new arrival from another part of the country, but we'd been attending the courses, conferences and events that the adviser ran for years. He and we were on first name terms and the same side.

During this mini-inspection, Mr Adviser sat in on a lesson I was doing with a low stream (streaming was rigid in the school) class. We were drawing pictures of characters from *Twelfth Night*, sticking them on a big sheet and then brainstorming single words to describe their characters which we added beneath the figures. Thus you might get 'drunk', 'rude' and fun' for Sir Toby Belch; 'lonely' and 'sad' for Olivia or 'moody' for Orsino. I honestly didn't think it was anything very special but my visitor seemed very taken with it.

I was by then applying for head of English posts. Three days after that lesson I found myself in a room with Mr Adviser again. It was an interview for a head of department position at a similar girls' school in Chatham. And he, bless him, was still enthusing about my efforts with the cut-out characters and their descriptors. Somehow he must have persuaded the others on the interview panel that I was the one and I got the job. Thank you, Mr Shakespeare.

As head of department, without a National Curriculum the world was my oyster and Shakespeare loomed large within it. I wrote an English department syllabus. There wasn't one when I arrived and there hadn't been one in my previous school. One of the things I included in it was a Shakespeare play each year and I specified which ones – not that it matters in the least whether you read *Macbeth* before *Julius Caesar* or *Romeo and Juliet* before *A Midsummer Night's Dream* but I wanted to ensure that each student got as wide a range as possible during her school years and that there was no repetition. There was also freedom for any teacher who wanted to do another play as well during the year provided it wasn't one which 'belonged' in another year and that the rest of my fairly fluid syllabus was covered.

On one occasion, the head of maths teased me incredulously saying: "Only you, Susan, could use Shakespeare as an incentive." I'd told him during staff room coffee chat that one girl had enjoyed doing *Twelfth Night* so much that she was sad when we finished it and asked me if we could do another Shakespeare play immediately. My response was that if we worked really hard and got everything else done there should be time to fit in another play before the end of term. At the same time I was organising as many trips to see the plays as possible and I like to think that students who passed though 'my' department during those years have happy memories of what fun we had with Shakespeare.

Meanwhile I'd hooked up with the Shakespeare in Schools Project run by Doctor Rex Gibson from Cambridge. There was a regular magazine and news of teachers all over the country making Shakespeare live for young people, although it still wasn't compulsory. Rex became editor of a series of Shakespeare texts published by Cambridge University Press and they too were sparky and attractive to use. His big thrust was the wonderful language which, he argued, should never be 'translated' but allowed to speak and sing for itself – with accessible glossary notes if necessary. Rex believed passionately that the language often doesn't need explaining. "No child needs to be told the meaning of 'when the hurly-burly's done'," he once told me.

I went on a ten-day course about teaching Shakespeare, led by Rex, at Girton College Cambridge in the late 1980s. He was a highly charismatic enthusiast who could quote almost every line of every play. Steeped in that language, if he went to a meeting with serious suited chaps at the Department for Education he'd twinklingly make them speak some Shakespeare with him. Wherever he went and whatever he did, love of Shakespeare flowed out of him continuously. And it was infectious.

During that course, he took us to London for the day where we stood in a group on the building site which was going to be Shakespeare's Globe and Rex made us chorus a speech together. Then we did the same thing at what's left of The Rose, round the corner from the Globe. We went to the Barbican and met the then head of RSC education and spoke more Shakespeare. He was like a clergyman praying with his flock – and after ten days I was even more besotted with Shakespeare, with a head full of ideas to try out in school and share with colleagues too.

In the 1980s I did an Open University degree – which I shall discuss in more detail in Chapter 9. One of the courses I opted for was, of course, Shakespeare: eight plays to study, talk and write about and, in my case, to see as often as I could in nine months. It was a joyous voyage, really getting inside *Hamlet*, *Anthony and Cleopatra*, *King Lear*, *Twelfth Night*, *Measure for Measure*, *Henry IV parts 1 and 2* and *The Tempest*. It was one of several courses for which I got a distinction based on the terminal exam and coursework.

Eventually I started to write professionally and, given my background, theatre reviewing was bound, sooner or later, to become part of the freelance mix. In the last thirty years or so I have reviewed productions of literally hundreds of Shakespeare plays and I reckon I have probably seen *Macbeth* fifty times – always with interest and curiosity. The joy of it is seeing what a director has done with this wonderful text, which can be interpreted in as many ways as there are people wanting to stage it.

Because I wanted to develop my second career as a writer, in 1993 I gave up full-time teaching and all the management responsibilities I had long shouldered. Instead I took a part-time position in a girls' boarding school where I taught a lot of A Level – which I'd never done before because almost all my previous experience was in eleven–sixteen schools.

Suddenly I was teaching Shakespeare at a whole different level and loving it. *Henry V* – ironically considering the miserable experience I'd had with it as my own O Level play – soon became my favourite A Level teaching text. There's so much humanity in the play. Yet was the titular monarch a war criminal? Shakespeare clearly thought he was and there's contemporary documentary evidence which proves that yes, he really did give the order for the murder of the French prisoners. So why does the Olivier 1944 film cut this altogether? Why does Kenneth Branagh's 1989 film change the order of the scenes? We had some fascinating, very informed classroom discussions. *Measure for Measure* was fun to teach too. Every teenage girl has strong views about the treatment of Isabella. We watched films and went to dozens of productions of texts we were studying. I eventually became allergic through over exposure to the Zeffirelli *Romeo and Juliet*. Even now the sound of the theme music sends me running in the opposite direction. I liked the Baz Luhrmann version, which one of the students brought in the days when we used VHS in classrooms. It seemed very refreshing by comparison.

I'm writing this chapter in May 2023. So far this year I have seen National Youth Theatre's *A Much Ado About Nothing* at Duke of York's Theatre, *Macbeth* at Southwark Playhouse, *Hamlet* at National Theatre and *The Tempest* at Shakespeare's Globe and reviewed them all. Coming up I have *Richard III* and another *A Much Ado About Nothing* – and there will be more. Since Covid there has been an upsurge in outdoor work by companies such as Half Cut and Illyria, and lots of small scale productions in pub and fringe theatres where economy of scale makes it viable – and as interesting as ever.

Yes, I am still in love with the world's finest, startlingly timeless playwright who has long loomed very large in my life.

5. TEACHING

The Silver Sword by Ian Seraillier

One of the best things the education department did in my three years at Bishop Otter College was to organise a children's books day. We were addressed by Rosemary Sutcliff, Brian Wildsmith and Ian Seraillier all of whom were, I think, fairly local to the college. And I was utterly fascinated. In fact, it's one of the very few education department projects that I remember at all. The rest of it has faded to lacklustre mush.

Rosemary Sutcliff, who died in 1992, had already published her famous 'Roman' trilogy, *The Eagle of the Ninth* (1954), *The Silver Branch* (1957) and *The Lantern Bearers* (1959) by the time I 'met' her in 1967. Later she wrote fine historical novels for children and young people, which humanised Arthurian legend and turned the characters into real people as opposed to the cardboard cut-outs I'd grown up seeing them as. Her books were nearly all historical and she was very prolific, working, evidently, right to the end of her life because five more books were published posthumously. Her obituaries say that she was writing on the morning that she died.

I had never, in 1967, read any of them but the most important lesson I learned from Miss Sutcliff that day was that a damaged or imperfect body does not mean an impaired mind. Don't judge me; I know it's obvious but my upbringing was pretty sheltered and I'd had almost no experience of people with impairments and disabilities. Rosemary Sutcliff had Still's Disease – a severe form of juvenile arthritis – and had used a wheelchair since early childhood. She came to Bishop Otter College, aged forty-something, with a companion/PA/carer who wheeled her in. She sat, her head a little large for her tiny body and her hands misshapen and immobile. She addressed us fluently, articulately and compellingly as she explained her research methods and the technology that she used to help her to write. I was both astonished and humbled.

Then came Brian Wildsmith. He was a painter by profession and had turned to illustration of children's books using vivid primary colours and dramatic geometric shapes. He had won the 1962 Kate Greenaway Medal for his wordless book *ABC*, five years before he came to Bishop Otter College to talk to us. Still then only in his thirties he had also done a glorious counting book and one about birds. Many more followed, including some delightful depictions of Bible stories. He died in 2016.

And finally there was Ian Seraillier whose work was later to loom large in my life. He wrote books for older children. To be honest I don't remember much of what he said that day but have learned since that he was a Quaker and member of the Peace Pledge Union who was granted conscientious objector status in World War Two. That explains the gentle humanity which runs through many of his books. He died in 1994. I wonder if he ever met Michael Morpurgo? They'd have had a lot in common.

It has long been a mystery to me why the staff at Bishop Otter didn't make much more of this excellent day. They should have told us, for example, to read at least one book by each of the three authors so that we'd come to the session with questions, thoughts and information. Of course they didn't. I had never heard of any of the three until I walked through the door to hear them speak.

Moreover, we should have been told to read at least one children's book a week. If we'd done that for three years we would have started our teaching careers with a really broad knowledge of current and recent work for young readers. There was so much going on. Alan Garner was stirring things up with his other-worldly novels such as *The Weirdstone of Brisingamen* (1960), *The Moon of Gomrath* (1963) and *The Owl Service* (1967) – all very different from the Enid Blyton and Eleanor M Brent-Dyer many of us recalled from our own quite recent childhoods. Philippa Pearce had won the 1958 Carnegie medal with *Tom's Midnight Garden* – a magical story about a lonely child able to hop into a time warp garden when the long case clock in the hall struck thirteen. *Charlie and the Chocolate Factory* arrived in 1964.

But in the event, nobody ever talked to us about children's books except on that one day. There was a school practice library which had sets of books students could borrow to take out with them on school practice. We should have been taken in there regularly and led to discover what was available so that we could educate ourselves in the literature available to the children we would soon be teaching – but we weren't. I don't remember reading a single children's book in the whole three years except *Episode of Sparrows* (arguably not a children's book at all) by Rumer Godden, which I had to take over as a class reader with an English class I was assigned on a teaching practice in Worthing in my second year. Of course, I might have worked out for myself how important this would be in the future but I was young and empty-headed and I didn't. I was a lot more focused on the enormous amount of 'grown up' reading I was doing in connection with my English main course which grabbed me much more than anything labelled 'education'. Maybe the fault was partly mine – but staff could have done much more and it would have been far more relevant than, say, playing with adding machines, which I remember once spending a whole morning on.

I did, however, have one more encounter with Ian Seraillier while I was still at college. He lived in nearby Singleton and had written a jolly story in music for the children in his local primary school to sing. He'd written the words but I'm afraid I can't remember who the composer was. A group of us musically-inclined students were asked to go to the school once a week to teach it to the children. Maybe it was a quid pro quo for Ian Seraillier's coming to the college. The school would have been used for teaching practice too so there must have been good contacts. Perhaps they didn't have a music teacher. Anyway, we went there several times in the college minibus driven by a slightly older student who happened also to be a fine pianist and the college organ scholar. The teaching was actually quite fun.

When I started teaching secondary boys in Deptford, aged twenty-one – my baptism of fire – I found *The Silver Sword* (1956) by Ian Seraillier in the English stock cupboard and fell upon it with relief. Here was something bearing a name I recognised. I hadn't read it at that point but took it home and devoured it in a single evening. Would these first year boys enjoy this? I thought they would and I was right: these and dozens of other classes I later taught in two more schools. It certainly went down better than the self-consciously twee *Emil and the Detectives* (1929) by Erich Kastner or *Black Ivory* (1948) by Norman Collins, a novel about illegal slave trading in 1829, both of which were in the same cupboard.

Re-reading *The Silver Sword* now after a long absence from it, I'm forcibly struck by the gentleness and decency of it. Anyone telling that story today would make it far grittier – but somehow Seraillier's emphasis on kindness doesn't diminish the book's power. Three Polish children escape from the Nazis who come for their dissident, Christian father who is a teacher. Both parents are taken to prison camps and the children set off across Europe, losing and then finding the eldest, Edek, along the way. They meet people who help them and those who don't. As the war ends they are determined to make for Switzerland where they hope, against all the odds, they might find their parents. So it's a quest story – full of delightfully drawn characters and dangerous adventures and terrible worries And the self-willed boy, Jan, they pick up on the way, is loveably rebellious having probably experienced unthinkable trauma on which Seraillier doesn't dwell. Because this is fiction, we get an unlikely happy ending and I found, with that first class I shared it with, that I couldn't read the final pages aloud without a tear and a catch in my voice. And I never could. Even as a septuagenarian returner I found myself welling up.

The Silver Sword was dramatised by Stuart Henson and twenty years after I'd first read the novel; I assistant-directed a production of it at the Kent girls' school I was by then teaching in. The story has never lost its power to move people. Later still there was a production at Polka Theatre in Wimbledon and I was invited as a journalist to sit in on a rehearsal. The actors told me how they remembered it from childhood and how strongly they identified with the characters. Soon (2026) *The Silver Sword* will be out of copyright after which anyone will be able to adapt it in anyway s/he chooses.

We saw Ian Seraillier's name a lot in the last decades of the 20th century. He and his wife, Anne, founded the 'New Windmill' series for Heinemann Books. They'd both been English teachers. There was a shortage of engaging, affordable reading material in schools and the series – durable, low budget hardbacks at paperback prices – aimed to rectify that. Heinemann Windmills were the backbone of every school English department in the country and I bet quite a number of them are still there. The huge list was extraordinarily eclectic too, ranging from, for example, Nigel Hinton's *Buddy* and Mary Norton's *The Borrowers* to Nevil Shute's *A Town Like Alice* and Chinua Achebe's *Things Fall Apart*. I have a 'New Windmill' copy of *Badger on the Barge* and other stories by Janni Howker (1984) in front me. At the back – as always – is listed other books in the series: 151 authors many of them with several titles. Many, like Seraillier's own books, were meant for children. Others, such as Harper Lee's *To Kill a Mockingbird* and DH Lawrence's *The Virgin and the Gypsy* clearly weren't but were used with older classes.

For me *The Silver Sword* was the start of a long project to immerse myself in children's literature and to communicate a love of reading to the students I worked with. Many studies have shown that children and young people who read for pleasure usually do better at everything else. I didn't need formal research. I knew it instinctively, particularly as I began to see the effects of taking reading seriously. As I was wont to tell students, with what I hoped was a friendly twinkle and only half joking: "People who read fiction know things."

Learning to read, I realised, is a two-stage process. First you have to learn to decode the squiggles. There are various approaches and I'm not going to debate the pros and cons of phonics here but eventually almost all children crack it, although some master it earlier than others.

Then you have to learn to read – really read. It takes practice to achieve the sort of effortless fluency which allows you to open a book and climb inside it. At some stage 'real readers' stop subvocalising or reading aloud to themselves in their head. Eventually the marks on the page learn to convert themselves into images, ideas, stories and information in the brain of the reader without any conscious route. It's pretty magical really. And it's what I spent much of my teaching career trying to develop – sadly there is still a tendency for teachers and parents to think that Ivy or Ivo can read now, aged six or seven, so we can just leave her or him to get on with it.

I soon worked out that many children don't see reading as grown-up behaviour. The adults in their lives, including teachers, tell them that now they have jobs and families they don't have time for reading (if they ever did). I worked for one Head who mentioned *David Copperfield* so often that I concluded it was probably the only book she'd ever read. And I've never forgiven Tony Blair for visiting a primary school early in his premiership and telling children who asked him about his favourite books that he was too busy to read. At consultation evenings I would gently ask parents who complained that their child didn't read about their own reading habits. I already knew the answer.

So one lesson a week was always devoted to independent reading. I didn't mind what they read as long as it was a proper book as opposed to a magazine or comic. And of course, I didn't sit at the front and do my marking. I read too. At the beginning of the lesson we all held our books up so that we could see each other's choices. I didn't choose an 'exemplar' book to read myself, either. I simply took whatever I happened to be reading. In the 1980s this was quite common and acquired acronyms such as ERIC (Everyone Reads in Class) or USSR (Uninterrupted Sustained Silent Reading). I suspect it's right out of fashion now – too simple and not interactive or bossy enough for Ofsted and how do you measure the outcomes? As I said, presciently as it turned out, to a school governor many years ago when he was quizzing me about 'quantifiable objectives': "If we're going to reduce education to that which can be measured then all is lost. Whoever it was who first pointed out that you don't fatten pigs by weighing them was spot on."

I continued my one lesson a week of independent reading for the rest of my thirty-six years in teaching – even in the boarding school when I taught part-time for my last eleven years. Sometimes I had to justify it to members of other departments to whom it looked like a cop-out but I could live with that. Developing, encouraging and celebrating reading is, in my view, the most important part of an English teacher's job.

That's why, once I was head of department, I launched an annual Books Week. It involved author visits – I knew some by then and people such as Bernard Ashley and Gillian Cross were a delight to host. Ideally these were evening sessions so parents could come too and we usually got a good turn-out thanks to my relentless (probably tiresome) enthusiasm with which I steamrollered everyone. I invited students, teachers and parents from other local schools too.

With the support of the Head, herself an English specialist, I manged to get whole school involvement in Books Week. I wanted the students to see that maths teachers and PE teachers read books and valued them too. It's not just an English teacher obsession. So I'd get a colleague from a different department to lead an assembly about a book he or she wanted to share. And I persuaded the Head to insist that tutor group time be devoted to ERIC for that week in all classes. We hooked up with a local bookshop, ran an all-day and all-evening book fair and invited parents.

Beyond Books Week, we also started a school bookshop, open every lunchtime, in a rather pretty garden shed in the foyer. In other words, I moved heaven and earth to put reading centre stage.

Not that it was always smooth sailing. In my first term as head of English I had a very cross phone call from a parent who thought the book I was reading with her daughter's class was Satanic. It was Leon Garfield's *The Ghost Downstairs* – an oblique reworking of the Faust legend. "Did you choose this book, Mrs Elkin?" she kept demanding angrily. I told her that I'd found copies in the stock cupboard that I'd just inherited and decided it was rather good. I also explained that Leon Garfield was a well-regarded and respected author. She then threatened me with Mr Palmer (not his real name). Palmer was the local vicar, one of our school governors and the Diocesan Exorcist. His assemblies were hair-raisingly extreme and had I been Head of that school I would have banned him from the premises. As it was, I simply told the agitated parent, as politely as I could, that it was I, as head of English, who decided which books were studied in my department, not Mr Palmer. I was relieved to hear no more about this from her, the Head or Mr Palmer.

In 1993 I took a part-time job in a girls' boarding school – of which more later. At my first parents' consultation meeting I met a father – let's call him Mr Carruthers. He'd obviously been quizzing his daughter about her new English teacher, "I can't tell you, Mrs Elkin, how delighted I am that at last Emma has an English teacher who likes reading," said Mr Carruthers.

I gulped in incredulity and replied, "Well I'd like to think that all English teachers are keen on reading but perhaps we'd better not go there..." He agreed that we shouldn't and went grinning on to the next teacher telling me over his shoulder to keep up the good work. He made my day, of course. Even when you know you're right it's good to have it confirmed.

6. VEGETARIANISM

Taking the Rough With the Smooth
by Andrew Stanway (1976)

So why did I become a vegetarian in 1978? Of course it all started with a book. And it was an indirect journey.

I have what medical practitioners delicately call a 'sluggish gut' and I've had it from infancy. By January 1976 I was concerned that my four-year-old, Lucas, seemed to be going the same way although, for the record, he assures me now that my worries were unfounded. So when I read a newspaper review of a new book called *Taking the Rough with the Smooth* which offered dietary solutions, I naturally was keen to learn more.

We were living in Wellingborough in Northamptonshire at the time and I went straight to the independent bookshop in Silver Street the next day and ordered it. There was no Internet, Amazon or Kindle to speed the process in 1976. The next week I collected it, read it and changed my life for ever.

Dr Stanway is a medically qualified doctor. A year younger than me, he was only twenty-eight when this pivotal book – several decades ahead of its time – was published. He went on to write other books about alternative medicine, mental health and eventually to focus mostly on sexual issues.

His argument, very well researched and convincing, was that we all need to eat more fibre. It was vital, he wrote, for gut health and could even assist weight loss. He made a strong case for wholemeal bread, wholewheat pasta (of which I'd never heard at the time), brown rice and pulses. It was also worth enhancing dishes with bran, he said, and cited medical studies from all over the world.

None of this sounds remotely original now that fibre content is given by law on every manufactured food and we all know that you're meant to have 30g per day. But in 1976, most people were scathing about 'roughage'. The prevailing view was that bran was indigestible by humans and therefore much better stripped out of our food and fed to cattle. Half a century later respected writers, doctors and researchers such as Tim Spector tell us that fibre is essential to feed the vitally important microbes in our gut which are crucial to our general health.

So where was I to buy what I needed to rectify my own gut problems? I knew you could buy wholemeal bread in any bakers because my maternal grandmother, who'd lived with us for most of my teens, was keen on it. So, I switched to it and have eaten no other sort of bread since. And incidentally the word 'brown' doesn't mean anything except to indicate colouring. Bread has to have the word 'whole' in the labelling to ensure that the bran which naturally surrounds the grain has been used.

I went to a health food shop – a new experience – which I found in a Wellingborough side street to find out what else was available. And there was the wholewheat – 'integrale' as the Italians call it – pasta, brown rice and many other things recommended by Dr Stanway. I stocked up and started experimenting. Quite soon my sluggish gut was a bit less sluggish.

Of course, I wasn't eating this food on my own. I was making family meals for the three of us. And as I was pregnant with my second child, Felix, who arrived in March 1976, we would soon be a family of four. I made spaghetti Bolognese with wholemeal pasta, curries with brown rice and baked with wholemeal flour. Lucas and I made lots of bread and he learned to help me knead it, standing on a chair in the kitchen in the time-honoured way.

Then I got curious. Most of this food related to plants. What else could I make? Vegetarians probably had some good ideas, I thought, so I went back to the bookshop to see what was on offer. I bought a very basic book: *500 Recipes Vegetarian Cookery* by Patty Fisher, sixth impression 1976. It cost 50p and I still have it. I have bought dozens of vegetarian cookery books since (and written recipe columns for magazines, myself) but Patty Fisher's was the first I read.

I had no intention of becoming a vegetarian at the time. I was still at the 'half a lamb jointed in the freezer' stage, along with chickens, pork chops and sections of beef all neatly stacked. I simply wanted wholefood inspiration. My only experience of vegetarianism was that I had a primary school friend who refused to eat meat (sixty-five years later she tells me she now eats organic meat). Then, during the Bishop Otter College trip to Stratford in 1968, I'd found and patronised a vegetarian restaurant for lunch a couple of times. I've always loved salad, derided by my father as 'rabbit food', and this little place near the theatre did some lovely ones. Beyond that vegetarianism just always seemed a way-out, rather cultish thing.

Patty Fisher had some interesting, very simple ideas. Nuts, for example, are another good source of fibre. I'd heard of nut roast. How on earth do you make it? I learned from Fisher that you have to make a thick gluey sauce with, say tomatoes and onions, into which you stir a mixture of ground nuts and breadcrumbs with herbs, garlic, chopped vegetables, spices and anything else you fancy including, maybe, beaten egg. Then you bake it in a loaf tin. The flavours and combinations are almost infinite. And if you get it right, it's delicious. So we started having it a lot. I made nut rissoles (refused to call them 'cutlets') which fried well too. Then there was something called 'nutty tatties' – mashed potato with nuts, the vegetarian answer to a fish cake. They became a family favourite.

My husband, incidentally, was well and truly on board with all this. Nick didn't share my sluggish gut problem but he liked the wholefoods which now underpinned our meals. Slowly over the next year or so we found ourselves buying and eating ever less meat because, in general, what we were having seemed so much more interesting and tasty. As a child, unlike most of my friends, I'd always found Sunday roast the most boring meal of the week but I loved the trimmings – mint sauce, onion sauce, apple sauce, stuffing and so on, depending what the meat was. Perhaps, had I but known it, the seeds (literally) of vegetarianism had lain dormant in me for a very long time. There was also a reluctant, terrified pig I watched being dragged and goaded, screaming and grunting into the back of a lorry at Dorchester Market when I was about ten and on holiday with my grandparents. I didn't quite make the connection with the food on my plate at the time but the very vivid image has remained with me.

In autumn 1977, with children aged five and eighteen months, we moved from Wellingborough to Kent because I had taken a full-time teaching job in Sittingbourne. I cooked a traditional Christmas dinner for the extended family in our new home and annoyed parents and in-laws by serving a wholemeal Christmas pudding and mince pies made with wholemeal flour. On one of those dead days between Christmas and New Year, Nick made an announcement: "I'm going fully vegetarian in the New Year," he said.

It took me about three months to join him partly because I hoped people, especially his parents, would realise that the two of us had made our decisions separately but it didn't work. It was viewed by everyone we knew as a corporate Elkin policy. The point was that by the beginning of 1978 we were down to eating meat and fish maybe once a fortnight. So we'd proved, although that wasn't what we'd set out to do, that we could live perfectly healthily without it. Once we'd recognised how unnecessary it was, all moral justification for the products of slaughter faded away and we were committed to it for ethical as well as health reasons. We told the children what we'd decided. No more meat would be served in our home but that they had a choice – if they wanted to eat meat dishes in other places that was entirely up to them. As they grew up, both rejected vegetarianism although Felix, whose wife is vegetarian, is now strictly non-meat and dairy for ethical reasons but he eats fish and eggs. He has come almost full circle.

Being vegetarian in the 1980s was not for the faint-hearted. It was unusual for a restaurant to offer a specific vegetarian option. Lunch time was easier than dinner because you could get a ploughman's in a pub but soup was doubtful unless you made it yourself because chefs love meat stock. You might be lucky and get offered an omelette but you couldn't bank on it. Even things such as roast potatoes were off limits because it was quite probable they'd been cooked in lard.

We had – and I still have – a policy of making the minimum fuss. Nonetheless there were a few occasions in restaurants when I was reduced to saying: "Look, I'm sorry to be difficult but could I just have two vegetable sides and a piece of cheese please?"

Indian restaurants were a real bonus and we all four developed a lasting passion for curry – mild dishes in my case. Because a substantial part of the Indian sub-continent (mostly the Buddhist and Hindu areas) is vegetarian anyway, there were, and are, lots of good vegetarian dishes in all UK Indian or Tandoori restaurants. I have been well nourished by things like tarka dahl, chana masala sag paneer many hundreds of times. After a while I even learned food-Hindi so that I know what the basic components of each dish are, although I'm well aware that I'm eating Anglicised, generic versions of these things. India is huge with many different cuisines. To talk of 'Indian food' is as silly as to refer to 'European food', as if spaghetti carbonara were the same as haggis or sauerkraut or anything like Yorkshire pudding. I was once lucky enough to be invited to dinner by a prosperous Muslim family of Indian extraction in Nairobi – parents of one of my students. The traditional dishes they proudly served bore no relation to what I was used to in my local UK Tandoori although some of the names were the same.

One learned things along the way too; Thai food is usually not good for vegetarians because their chefs tend to rely heavily on fish sauce. Chinese food, which I used to love in pre-vegetarian days, often contains bits of meat even when it's labelled as a vegetable dish. The French seemed, at least in the 1980s, to have no concept of vegetarianism. If you tried to explain they simply looked astonished and said, "*Mais, pourquoi?*" In the home of a French friend I was once firmly told, "*Aujourd'hui tu manges normalement, Susan.*" Of course I didn't – I just ate her delicious vegetables but it was awkward. Germany is a vegetarian desert. Austria is better. In 1993 Lucas went to Argentina with the Kent County Youth Orchestra. "Don't ever go to South America, it's all beef. You'd starve," he said when he got back. So I never have.

The other problem with 1980's vegetarianism was the attitude of the wider family. My parents thought we were mad but more or less accommodated our new way of life, mostly with respect even though it was a nuisance. It was different with the in-laws with whom we never again ate a Christmas dinner or Sunday lunch. My mother-in-law blamed me for brainwashing her son and making him 'cranky' – completely ignoring the fact that he had a mind of his own and was more than capable of making independent decisions irrespective of anything I thought or said. It was particularly hurtful not to be invited to Nick's aunt's silver wedding lunch in a hotel in Surrey because her sister, my mother-in-law, had told her that we were impossible to feed and would be embarrassing guests. Of course, even in 1979 the hotel would have provided something for us if they'd been told in advance. Once said aunt was widowed, the following year, she invited us over regularly for lunch, gave us non-meat food which she seemed to enjoy herself, and it wasn't any sort of issue. She often came to us and happily ate what I cooked too. I wonder if she regretted listening to her blinkered sister and not including us at that party?

In the end I took to inviting Nick's parents for Sunday tea, which seemed to be the only meal we could share without acrimony. I'd make cakes, scones and sandwiches and it was reasonably amicable. Sometimes, however, it wasn't. On one occasion my mother-in-law's elderly uncle was staying with them and they were coming to visit us. "I'll bring a cake because your cake might make Uncle John ill," she told me blithely, leaving me in the white heat of astonished fury. In the event they arrived cake-less. Instead, she brought me a rather beautiful cardigan/jacket which I wore for several years. I reckon George, my mild father-in-law, had asserted himself for once and said something on the lines of, "Do you want to alienate Susan completely? Be reasonable." So I accepted the peace offering with as much grace as I could muster and Uncle John happily ate two slices of my cake.

After my mother-in-law's death in 2004, we spent much more time with George who, obviously, now needed extra companionship. He ate whatever I gave him and always enjoyed a second helping of my cheese-topped lentil shepherd's pie. I chuckled when Felix reported that George had said to him, "I really quite like your mum's vegetarian food." It only took thirty-five years.

Our move to Kent back in 1977 was primarily to get Nick out of a job which he loathed and which was affecting his health. He was now what used to be called a 'house husband' and that was pretty rare in 1977. It meant that he looked after the children while I taught. Money was tight but we muddled through and he seemed a lot happier. But he had got really caught up in the whole healthy eating/vegetarian way of life and wanted to start a business. To be honest I was never very keen on this plan. I didn't think he was cut out for it. I had grown up in a family business run by entrepreneurial self-employed people. He hadn't. And, predictably, his mother was horrified. She was upset enough that, as she saw it, he wasn't working whereas I was on some sort of ego trip. She hated anything remotely resembling a healthy food item and was particularly dismissive of sesame seeds for some reason. The last thing she wanted was her only child doing anything as demeaning as running a business. (She was generous in other ways, though, and had helped us to buy the house in Kent which we wouldn't otherwise have been able to afford.)

So gradually in 1978, Harvest Home Wholefoods (proprietors Nicholas and Susan Elkin) was born. Initially Nick wanted a shop but none of the premises we looked at worked out, thank goodness. We would have lost a lot of money that we didn't have. I refused even to discuss re-mortgaging the house in order to raise capital. I told Nick and the children that I would never, ever sign anything which might jeopardise the roof over our heads. In the end he decided to do it as a market stall because that didn't require much outlay. We'd had a fairly decent car, passed on to us cheaply by his parents when they replaced theirs, which was now sold to buy a dreadful, unreliable yellow Bedford van which I was terrified to drive – in fact I remember only two occasions when I took it out on my own. Later he had a big Datsun estate car bought from my uncle who let us pay in instalments. That was a much better option as far as I was concerned.

He found out where to buy wholesale wholefoods and stocked up – mainly from a place called Community Wholefoods in Southgate in North London. Later he met Alex and Chiara Smith who founded Alara Wholefoods in 1977. They were squatters in

Tolmer Square near Euston Station when Nick first found them. They made wholefood no-sugar muesli there and Nick bought it to sell on. Later they had shops. Today Alara is a major supplier to supermarkets. Nick bought Bombay Mix first from a unit in Covent Garden and later from a scruffy factory on an industrial estate where the chaps always gave sweets to pre-school Felix, who usually had to be taken along on these trips. Bombay Mix was one of Nick's most popular lines because customers said it was always crisp and never stale.

The Harvest Home Wholefoods vehicle, whichever one it was, was packed with trays of fresh herbs and spices, bags of pulses, nuts, seeds, dried fruits, rice, pasta and a lot more. The big sacks were stored in our cellar at home where Nick, and one of my students who did it as a Saturday job, spent hours weighing out and bagging up. After each retail day Nick would stock-take and make a list of what needed to be replaced in the trays for the next one. Also in the vehicle, or on its roof, were the poles which made up a market stall: the big tarpaulin, the table, the big clips to hold it all together and a lot more.

The best market he ever did was Sevenoaks on a Wednesday. Over time he built up a regular customer base and people said his herbs and so on were deliciously fresh. On the way home, after the market closed down at about 4.00pm, he delivered to some of his elderly customers who couldn't carry what they wanted. In the end, one or two of these would regularly phone their orders through to him at home so that he could have their shopping bagged up ready rather than taking it off the stall. During the seven years that Harvest Home Wholefoods existed, he also ducked in and out of markets in Herne Bay, Ashford, Sittingbourne, Maidstone Tonbridge, Faversham, among other Kent towns.

The events which paid best were craft fairs and boot fairs, of which we did quite a number, and it was 'we' because things like the Faversham May Day fair or an annual event in Dover Town

Hall tended to be on bank holidays so we all went – with a curry treat at the restaurant at the bottom of our road in the evening if we'd done well.

I worried about the way the business leaked money but because it was what Nick really wanted to do, I did everything I could to support him. Bearing in mind that the checks on domestic kitchens were nothing like as stringent then as they are now, I used to make things for Nick to sell on the stall. For a one-off craft fair I'd do big trays of sticky gingerbread or fruit cake, which always sold well at a good profit because the ingredients had come in wholesale though the business. Cheese scones were my speciality and I made a couple of big batches for each market day – getting up very early in the morning to get them done before school. Sometimes at Sevenoaks there would be people waiting for him to unload in order to buy my wholemeal cheese scones.

We also did talks about wholefood eating and those tended to fall to me because I've been standing up in front of people all my life but Nick was not a natural public speaker. Once an educator, always an educator, I suppose. I spoke at WI groups, clubs, organisations and anyone who asked me. I remember doing one talk at the annual Broadstairs Folk Festival which seems unlikely but there was a good audience. I would talk about the principles of wholefood eating, how you can get protein from non-animal sources and what health benefits might come from eating various plant foods – always making it clear that I was a cook running a wholefood business not a qualified nutritionist. At the end of the talk, our goods were available for sale and it usually worked pretty well.

The other thing I did was to run vegetarian cookery courses at home for three to six people on Saturdays, mostly recruited from market stall customers. Nick would take the children out for the day and come home at about 3.30pm in time to sell wholefoods to anyone who wanted them. As a talking point I put display cookery books all around the space we used as a kitchen diner. When the participants arrived I'd serve coffee and wholemeal biscuits made in advance and we'd chat about food. Then, collaboratively, we'd make Rose Eliot's red kidney bean and tomato quiche which we'd share for lunch with salad. After lunch we'd prepare a sticky prune and molasses cake together which was eaten with a cup of tea at the end of the day. I provided recipe sheets and many of them took notes. Tips, ideas and information were shared all day. These courses were actually one of the most successful things Harvest Home Wholefoods did because the overheads were low and each person paid a reasonable course fee. Over fifty people attended overall so I like to think I more than did my bit for the wholefood/vegetarian cause.

How on earth I found the energy to teach all day, make the scones and do these talks and courses at other times, I have no idea. I was also doing a fair amount of private coaching in the evenings because we never had any money. What you can juggle in your thirties seems unimaginable a few decades later.

Vegetarianism became an easier lifestyle to manage in the 1990s and early 2000s as gradually many of the foods we needed went mainstream and began to appear in supermarkets. That was what finally finished Harvest Home Wholefoods, of course. It couldn't compete once you could buy our herbs, spices, beans and the like at supermarket prices. We didn't fail. We helped put it on the map. We were pioneers – part of a movement and we succeeded.

Restaurants improved enormously too. The trade soon recognised that a significant proportion of their customers wanted vegetarian food so they started catering for them. Mad cow disease (spongiform bovine encephalopathy) was a factor too. It can lead to an appalling, invariably fatal, variant in humans called Creutzfeldt-Jakob disease. It's pretty rare but publicity in the 1990s frightened people and triggered a shift away from beef and beef products such as rennet in cheese.

Moreover, vegetarian food is often very nice – not cranky, weird, tasteless or boring – and many people, who make no claim to vegetarianism, will often choose it for an occasional change. Soon, therefore, there was at least one 'veggie' option on almost every restaurant menu and for people like me it felt like a happy home coming.

Ironically, it has become more difficult again now. There has been a huge upsurge in what I call 'aggressive veganism'. It's all linked with very justified animal welfare concerns and anxiety about climate change. Of course I understand where vegans are coming from and fully accept that my own position as a lacto-vegetarian is illogical. I am not complacent but, like Bernard Shaw, I'm quite pleased to think of the long line of cows, pigs, sheep, chickens and fish whose death I haven't caused in the forty-five years that I've been vegetarian. In all that time, though, I have never proselytised or been judgemental about anyone else's ethical food choices. Sadly there's a new wave of millennial vegans who take a different view and I don't think it helps their cause.

Restaurants, understandably, often take the easy way out because they want to keep it simple. Many of them no longer offer vegetarian choices. Instead there are plenty of vegan options. From the restaurant's point of view, any vegetarian can eat vegan food so that's both boxes ticked. The trouble is that too often now 'plant based' means ultra-processed, very unhealthy synthetic food such as burgers made with chemical additives and unrecognisable ingredients, rather than vegetables, which are often reduced to things such 'carrot essence' whatever that may be. Supermarkets are full of them too because veganism has become big business. Tim Spector argues very cogently in his book *Food for Life: The New Science of eating* (2022) that ultra-processed foods (USPs) are responsible for many of our health issues including diabetes, heart disease and obesity.

In restaurants now I often go for main course salads because I can see the tomatoes, leaves, nuts and the like so it's all fairly true to the wholefood principle I've lived by since 1976. And I avoid anything styling itself as 'plant based'. I'd rather have plants.

I still have my battered, tattered copy of *Taking the Rough with the Smooth* – probably the most significant life-changer I have ever read.

7. LOVE

Down and Out in London and Paris
by George Orwell (1940)

The church youth club at St Paul's Church, Forest Hill was my social life and my springboard. It was run by a couple of teenagers three or four years older than me who invited my friend, Susie, and me along when we were thirteen. The club alternated between the church hall and people's homes. Table tennis, records on the turntable, chats, and tea were the order of the day. There was a lot of smoking but I don't remember any boozing. The association with the church was almost incidental because there was nothing earnest or preachy about it.

As it happens, I was a regular church-goer at that point in my life. My grandparents had been committed to St Paul's all their married life and my paternal grandfather, William Hillyer, was church warden there for many years. He always read the first lesson at Evensong too. The old church in Waldenshaw Road was bombed during the war after which the church moved into a modern, formerly non-conformist, building in Taymount Rise and that is what I remember. The old bombsite was still there in the early 1960s; the youth club got permission to hold firework parties on it at least twice. That land is now part of Sainsburys and its car park. The Taymount Rise church was eventually deconsecrated and converted to flats.

For me the youth club was a life-changer because members inevitably brought friends along. That meant there were new faces every week and the club grew very quickly. I was a pupil in a pretty old fashioned all girls' grammar school. I don't think I'd spoken to a boy since primary school and now suddenly I was meeting boys from all the local schools every week: Alleyn's, Dulwich College, Brockley County, Archbishop Tennyson's, Kingsdale and more. Nobody talked much about hormones when I was thirteen but I suppose mine were kicking in. I was awestruck like Miranda in *The Tempest*: 'O brave new world, That has such people in't !'

Inevitably there was pairing off although I was a shy, gauche, prickly sort of teenager and very little of that came my way although there were plenty of conversations. I've never been a pop music person, having adored classical music almost from infancy, but if I hear even a bar or two of the Everly Brother's 'Cathy's Clown', Roy Orbison's 'Three Steps to Heaven' or anything by Adam Faith, Buddy Holly or Cliff Richard I'm transported instantly back to that dusty church hall, the smell of the steaming urn and the click of snooker balls as the boys played at one end of the room.

One of the youth club's projects was to raise money to refurbish the pretty awful church hall kitchen. To this end we staged some very amateurish Christmas entertainments which we jokingly called 'Saturday Night at the St Pauladium' because *Sunday Night at the Palladium* was a hugely popular TV show. There were a number of musicians and aspirant directors amongst us so it wasn't too difficult to get items together – usually led by the church organist who was an Alleyn's boy a year older than me. He was very talented but dogged by what I think, looking back, was probably schizophrenia. Years later, as an adult, it led to his living permanently in an institution.

I could sing quite well in those days and one of my party pieces was a take-off of Shirley Bassey. My version was called Burley Chassis. My mother had helped me make an outlandish dress from an old yellow bedspread. I sang 'As Long as He Needs Me' with silly words and a version of the *Goldfinger* theme called 'Fishfinger'. I also had to lead community singing which involved a rapid change of clothes. To cover this one of boys did a Liberace spot and played Handel's 'Largo' on piano more slowly than it's ever been played by anyone, ever. And if I still wasn't ready, he played it again even slower. One show ended with our version of 'I'm Dreaming of a White Christmas'. It went: 'I'm dreaming of a new kitchen / with cupboards new and paintwork clean / where the sink units glisten and paint ain't missin'/ in great big patches from the wall. Please make this just not a pipe dream/ By supporting the youth club's kitchen scheme.' It was huge fun and in the end the kitchen was done up. And I've never been able to remember the words that Bing Crosby actually sang.

One day in the spring of 1962, when I was fourteen, the club was meeting at the home of two sisters who were pupils at James Allen Girls School (universally known, then and now, as JAGS). Their father was a dentist and their mother a sports car-driving flirt. They were wealthier than most of us. Across the room was a slight boy with thick, gingery brown hair, wearing a finely checked sports jacket and looking a bit ill at ease. I'd never seen him before.

"Who's that?" I asked the girl next to me.

"Oh, that's Nick," she said. "He's a friend of David's." He was sixteen, almost exactly two years older than me.

I don't remember speaking to him that evening but over the next few months he gradually became part of the crowd and we used to chat a lot. Then he started calling on me at home and I went to his home and met his parents. He lived less than a mile from me. When I think about it now, I suspect he fancied me from the very start. I had a lot of long, lustrous dark hair which he used to talk about dreamily, years later after I'd cut if off. At the time I thought we were just friends and I'd learned the word 'platonic' at school which seemed to fit the bill. He was, though, a very diffident young man and he'd had an unfortunate experience (I never knew exactly what) with another girl which had made him even more chary. So there was never anything remotely resembling what my grandmother would have called a 'pass'. It would be over five years before we got to that.

Instead we talked and talked – often about classical music. He was a geeky, quite knowledgeable music lover and I was playing and discovering lots of music at school and elsewhere so we had interests in common. After a while – a great compliment – he decided that I could be trusted to treat his precious LPs with appropriate respect and started lending them to me. That was how I first heard all the major violin concertos. By the time I was in the sixth form I was buying Proms tickets and offering the second ticket to friends and often that meant Nick. I vividly remember the one at which I heard *The Rite of Spring* for the very first time. I'd chosen that concert because I wanted to hear the Brahms violin concerto which preceded it. He was very excited about the Stravinksy, a composer who was new to me at that point. When I played a solo Prokofiev piece in the senior concert at school, Nick was there in the audience to support me. He had nothing to do with 'Saturday Night at the St Pauladium' but he was quietly in the back row to see his friend strutting her stuff.

Something odd happened at home too. "Did you say that boy's name is Elkin?" asked my father one day. "I bet that's Roy's or George's son." It turned out that my father and his brother, Terry, were very close friends with Nick's father and uncle before the war. They were all in the same Scout troop. In fact, my uncle and Nick's father had been best friends. Yes, South London was just a village and to a certain extent still is. Eventually we got them all together again and they remained pals for the rest of their lives. Thus, in a sense, the person who became the love of my life was almost the boy next door.

When I was sixteen or seventeen, Nick shyly gave me a birthday present – pretending it was nothing. The gift was the new Penguin edition of *Down and Out in Paris and London* by George Orwell. It was tersely inscribed in tiny writing: 'Happy Birthday, N.' I was rather flattered. There was a frisson in having a male friend like this and no boy had ever bought me a birthday present before. I wonder how long he'd thought about it and how long it had taken him to pluck up the courage? He had just discovered Orwell through doing *Animal Farm* for O Level and was very taken with it – he was dabbling with East Dulwich Young Socialists at the time and I went to a couple of meetings with him. That present was my introduction to Orwell and I soon read most of his other titles including, of course, *Nineteen Eighty Four*, a date we were still twenty years off reaching in 1964. Later Nick and I shared many books but *Down and Out in Paris and London* was the first.

When I went to Bishop Otter College Chichester to train as a teacher in 1965 the old crowd from home were regular weekend visitors. Sometimes they came singly and sometimes in groups. If you could find someone of the right sex (hostels were strictly segregated) who was going away for the weekend you could, if he or she was agreeable, book their room for your visitor. All you then had to do was get clean sheets from the domestic bursar and pay a modest charge for laundry. It worked well and that's how most of my visitors, including Nick, were accommodated although we also used the B&B places in town.

The really good thing about this was that because my friends were mostly two or three years older than me, they had acquired cars by now and it was lovely to have the freedom to explore further afield. There was an occasion when a group of us went to a night club in Hayling Island for example – one of only two occasions that I ever saw Nick drunk. Afterwards in the small hours we went to a bowling alley and he knocked all the skittles down with his first ball, which most people don't manage even when they're stone cold sober. I have happy memories of being driven to the 'big' cinema in Brighton too, which is where I first saw *Doctor Zhivago*, still my favourite film of all time.

Nick, however, didn't yet have a car. When I first met him he had a moped which took him everywhere, clad in his brown faux leather bomber jacket and crash helmet. It was really only one step up from a push bike and a joke in comparison with the big menacing machines then being pounded down to Margate by Mods and Rockers. When he was seventeen or eighteen he progressed to a Heinkel bubble car. Because it had only three wheels you could drive it on a motorcycle licence. It was a serviceable enough vehicle for two, or even three, people. On one occasion he drew up outside our house and my father watched in amazement as it disgorged five people. Perhaps that sort of abuse was why it finally failed its MOT and had to be written off because the tester, who could see big holes in the floor, refused even to get in it.

During most of my first two years at college Nick remained car-less but he took and passed a standard driving test so that he could occasionally borrow his parents' Morris Traveller. When he came to Chichester, though, it was by train or as a passenger in someone else's car. That all changed in 1967.

Nick finished his teacher training course at St Marks and St John's in Chelsea in the summer of 1966 but had by then decided that he definitely didn't want to teach. He was right. He'd have hated it and I doubt that he'd have been very successful at it. The mystery – and even he could never explain – is why he went to teacher training college in the first place and stuck to it for three years. I remember, as early as 1964, his father, George, saying to me that he couldn't see Nick ever teaching. I sat politely in their sitting room, aged seventeen, incredulously wondering why on earth, in that case, he was at college. Of course, there were grants and free tuition in those days. No one would drift like that now that you have to pay dearly for every moment of higher education. The only gain, that I could ever see, was that it left him with life-long detailed knowledge of the back streets and short cuts in Fulham and Chelsea, which he negotiated daily for three years on his moped or bubble car having ridden or driven there from Forest Hill. Useful, for example, when he often had to meet me after Society of Authors meetings in Drayton Gardens in the early noughties.

When he left college he went to work as an admin assistant at Lewisham Borough Council. His social worker mother arranged it through someone she knew at the Town Hall. It would of course have been much better if he'd done this when he left school at eighteen but you can't rewrite history. Because he was bright he soon learned a lot about local government through the placements he was put on in a wide range of departments over the next year or two.

It meant that he now had a salary. And I discovered long after that, from his very first pay cheque, he started saving with Lambeth Building Society with a view to setting up home, by implication with me. He bought a car too – an old grey Morris 1000 with a low mileage which had belonged to a retired nurse acquaintance of his mother's. Now mobile, he needed somewhere to go on his new wheels so suddenly he seemed to be making regular beelines for Chichester at weekends. Still, as far as I understood, just good friends, he and I spent much of the summer term exploring Sussex, Hampshire and even Dorset, always my favourite county. It suddenly felt very grown up to be able to do such things independently of adults.

After one particularly long day out he said that we'd really driven too far. If I wanted to visit places like that again, perhaps we could stay away overnight? It seemed a good idea and we agreed to go to Bath and up the Wye Valley for three days early in the summer holiday. When I got home I casually told my mother about this plan. A few hours later she said, clearly intrigued and having had time to think about it, "Did you say you were going away with Nick next week?" Realising what she was thinking, I simply muttered an affirmative and closed the conversation down.

That mini-holiday was very pleasant but tense. Of course, we had separate rooms. We stayed two nights in the Vicarage at Wells where the vicar's wife did B&B and she clearly thought us a lovely, chaste couple. We were chaste all right but not yet a couple. Nick was so nervous that I don't think he ate more than a mouthful for the whole time we were away. I loved the 'sylvan' Wordsworthian Wye Valley which was new to me. Nick had been there on a Scout camp.

When we got back to London, he fell into the habit of coming round almost every night and we'd drive out to a country pub for a drink and maybe a walk. I had worked out by then that – almost incredibly – things were changing. He was always there. He was getting more tactile too – lots of arm and shoulder patting – and that was new.

Then on the 14th of August, the night before I was due to go away with my parents on a five-week tour of France including a Folk Festival and singing/playing spots in Dijon, Nick and I went to a Prom. I stupidly forgot the tickets. We sorted it with the box office somehow but I was embarrassed, upset and annoyed with myself. He put his arm round me and told me to stop worrying. Then, after the concert, when we got back to my family home (they were all out) I made hot drinks and we sat in the sitting room where he inched closer and closer. Suddenly I was in his arms and we were an item. It was five and half years since our first meeting.

Then I had five weeks in France to think about it. Was this really what I wanted? Yes, definitely. I'd been on a slow burn, hardly daring to think that it was really happening, but I was there now. I'd seen my future and I was very happy about it.

I returned in mid-September to a man who'd had to deal with a few things in my absence. His parents had taken their caravan to Germany where his father, George, then aged only forty-two, had had some sort of heart emergency. Panic stations. Nick, who was an only child, had to fly out and take charge. Aged twenty-two, he'd never been in an aircraft, never driven on the right and never towed a caravan. But he rose to the challenge and got them home safely. When I next saw George he was still in bed recovering under the supervision of his own doctor back home in Forest Hill. And in those days when there were no mobile phones or internet and few people made international calls, I knew none of this until I got home.

Nick drove me and my luggage back to college in place of my father who usually did this job and we saw each other every weekend for the whole of my third year – getting ever closer and more committed to a shared future. Within weeks, despite Nick's reticence, we were lovers in every sense of the word. Now when he came to Chichester, he brought his tent and we used to camp out so that we could be together all night – the rule was that men had to leave the women's hostels (and vice versa) by 11.00pm. We got engaged early in 1968 and were married the following year a few months after I'd left college and started work.

I read a lot throughout all this, obviously, and was a bit puzzled to find that Nick didn't – or not much, anyway. He was, for example, amazed to see that I'd put a book in my suitcase (it was a Gore Vidal novel) when we went on our honeymoon to Paris. I'm surprised, thinking back, that for nine days away I'd packed only one. Gradually, though, he started to read more and eventually he was reading as habitually as me partly because we didn't have TV for several years after we were married. And even when we succumbed it was a small portable which lived in a cupboard. In the end we got digital TV like everyone else but to this day I have only one small screen in the sitting room – the sort of thing others have in their bedrooms – and it's not on for more than three or four hours a week.

Before we downsized from our big house in Sittingbourne, with its fifty-two stairs, I reckon we had five thousand books with bookcases on every landing and round all walls in one upstairs room. Of course there had to be serious culling in order to shoehorn ourselves into our small, suburban, three-bedroom semi in 2016, back 'home' in SE London. I got it down to about a thousand volumes keeping everything we really wanted (like that beloved copy of *Down and Out in Paris and London*), all the poetry, Shakespeare and books about writing. Otherwise, I decided, if I wanted to re-read anything I could simply rebuy it in paperback or download it on Kindle. And that's what I did and do.

Kindle, of course, made a huge difference to Nick's reading and mine because the account was in my name with his device as 'Susan's second Kindle'. I bought books all the time and he simply hit the download button and read what I'd ordered. In a way it was like his parents all over again. Mollie would bring books home from the library and George would read them. Rarely did my father-in-law choose one for himself and Nick was the same – unless, for example, we were in a bookshop and something really caught his eye.

The wonderful thing about sharing Kindles is that you can read the same book at the same time and we often did – none of that waiting impatiently for the other person to finish the book you were itching to get your hands on. And of course we discussed them. I remember watching him reading *Fingersmith* by Sarah Waters (2002) and waiting for him to jump and say "Oh!" when he got to the best plot twist in modern literature. And of course he didn't disappoint me.

One thing Nick was very good at was vetting titles for me. I have always hated holocaust fiction and anything to do with torture or graphic violence. My mother knew how it would upset me and would sometimes gently say when she'd finished a book: "I don't think you'd like that one, Susan," and I always heeded her warnings. It was kindly protection from someone who knew me well rather than censorship. Once we were married and sharing books all the time, Nick took over that role. He'd read something either in a print copy or, later, on Kindle, and say darkly, "Don't read that one," so I didn't – and thus usually managed to avoid nightmares.

There was one occasion, though, when we came unstuck together. We'd both read *Therese Raquin* by Emil Zola without feeling especially distressed so were quite interested to see the 1980 TV adaptation which got nominated for awards. We hadn't got far before the adulterous couple were being graphically haunted by the drowned corpse of the murdered husband. We sat in chilled, clammy silence until he said (one of us had to say it first), "Shall we turn this off?" Later that night I was tossing and turning and aware that Nick was awake. "Are you thinking about that TV thing?" he asked eventually. By mutual agreement we turned on the bedroom lights and I went downstairs in search of comforting hot drinks. The BBC used to refer to wimps like us as 'people of a nervous disposition'.

When Nick was dying in Lewisham hospital in 2019 one of the staff asked where we met. I told her, turned to Nick and asked him if he remembered the youth club. "Of course I do," he replied with a vehemence which had largely left him by then. That youth club was certainly pivotal and in some ways has stayed with me all my life. I still hear from Susie. Although she and I were at primary school together she went to a different grammar school from me. She too found the love of her life at the youth club. She married her own Alleyn's boy five months after our own wedding and they remain happily married fifty-four years (at the time of writing) later. Nick and I stayed in touch with several other youth club friends who were also his school friends. One has died but I still see two of them. Today, of course, they are elderly chaps with lots of grandchildren.

8. CHILDREN

Clever Polly and the Stupid Wolf by Catherine Storr (1955)

Imagine a campsite in the South of France on a warm August evening. French families are cooking their supper so there's a whiff of smoke, red wine and garlic in the balmy air along with the clunking sound of Gallic chaps playing boules and children of various nationalities cheerfully enjoying tag together because it doesn't need language.

Then suddenly from one small tent, owned by an English family, come peals and peals of spontaneous infantile laughter – so loud and unexpected that for a few seconds everyone stops what they're doing and listens. What on earth is going on?

Felix was five and we'd decided that he should go to bed – it was already two hours after his usual bedtime. So we'd showered him in the wash block in lieu of the bath he would have had at home and Nick had crawled into the little tent the boys slept in to read Felix his bedtime story. The book was *Clever Polly and the Stupid Wolf* and that was the source of all that joyful hilarity.

Catherine Storr, who died in 2001, originally wrote these stories for her own daughters. There were eventually four volumes of them and they've never been out of print. I have *The Complete Adventures of Clever Polly and the Stupid Wolf* (Puffin, 2016) on my desk in front of me. Polly is a feisty, sensible little girl constantly harassed by a very anthropomorphic wolf who wants to eat her up. He disguises himself, lies and invents tricks but she sees through him every single time. And it's funny because every child knows that in fairy stories the dastardly, cunning wolf usually wins and gets to scoff a piglet or kid or two, or even the occasional granny. But not this wolf because he's too dim. The stories make me laugh even now that I'm two generations on.

Yes, they're a bit dated. People use threepenny bits, have their meat delivered by a butcher and wear mackintoshes but somehow that adds to the charm rather than detracting from it. Felix tells me that he read the stories so much to his own daughters that his original childhood copy just fell apart. In the end he had to buy a Kindle download so that he could go on fulfilling the demand. And that's another special thing about books loved in childhood – you can hand the joy on to the next generation like a precious gift.

I became a mother, aged twenty-four, three years after Nick and I were married when Lucas arrived in January 1972. He was born in our flat in Forest Hill because the birth was all set to be straightforward and that was our preferred option. I have vivid memories of inching myself out of bed at 2.00am because I thought that maybe, at last, something was happening. So I quietly made tea and sat at the kitchen table reading *The Forsyte Saga* waiting to see if the signs got stronger. Then Nick woke, realised I wasn't there, and staggered out to the kitchen.

"What's going on?" he asked.

"Well I think I might be having a baby," I told him, sarcastically. He then offered to boil lots of hot water because that's what you're supposed to do at this moment – isn't it?

Gosh, we were young and ignorant. If there were NCT groups back then no one told us about them. And I wasn't offered ante-natal classes so I got books from the library which built on my zoology A Level and gave me a detailed account of foetal development. Otherwise it was advice from my mother and grandmother and do your own thing. Nick rang the midwife at 7.00am but told her he didn't think there was any hurry so she said she'd get her children to school and then come up. In the event her assistant arrived at 8.30am and had to go into speedy action. Then the midwife herself joined us followed by Lucas before 11.00am. They didn't even have time to bring in the gas and air.

I was a good breast feeder and neither of my children ever had a bottle but goodness it's a boring business. So, of course, I read at the same time, holding the book in whichever hand wasn't supporting the baby in position. Two of the books I read during Lucas's first weeks were Daphne du Maurier's *Hungry Hill* and *The Mill on the Floss*. I had the latter (and still have it) in a small format Oxford Classics Edition so it was easy to hold in one hand.

My mother wanted me to establish a routine of four hourly feeds. It was a bit old fashioned but I more or less managed it with baby pit stops at 10.00, 2.00, and 6.00 both day and night. The reading was particularly useful at 2.00am because I was terrified of falling asleep and crushing him so I always got up and sat in a chair in another room – with book and tea tray to hand. Lucas quite quickly dropped the 10.00pm feed but continued to wake at 2.00am for three months, after which he slept ten to twelve hours through the night. I've never been sure whether this was luck or management. I suspect that a fairly rigid routine leads to established sleep patterns more quickly. I watch young mothers now, run ragged by demand feeding and sleepless nights and think that perhaps my way was better but it's not helpful to tell them that especially as it flies in the face of everything the 'experts' now tell them.

Soon I was taking my baby to the library. At eighteen months he had his own library ticket and we would browse picture books and take them home. We also had a lot of books of our own. One of his favourites for bedtime when he was about three was Dick Bruna's *Tilly and Tessa*. I read it aloud so many times that I could almost do it from memory, even now. He also liked the Ladybird version of *Chicken Licken*, given to him by some well-meaning relation, which Nick and I both loathed – banal and silly. We kept hiding it but Lucas always found it.

Libraries, by the way, were nothing like as child-friendly in the 1970s as they should have been. Forest Hill library, which was quite spacious, refused to let me take the pram in. There had recently been a very high profile baby snatching case nearby in Bromley which concentrated the mind of every young mother in the country so I certainly wasn't going to leave Lucas outside in his pram as previous generations would have done. When I complained about this to one librarian he said: "Well you'll just have to come in the evening without the baby when your husband's at home." He'd probably lose his job for saying that now.

By the time Felix was born in March 1976 we were living in Wellingborough in Northamptonshire because Nick's employer, the Local Government Training Board, had relocated from the Albert Embankment in London to the Arndale Centre in Luton and they paid for our move. There were a few last-minute complications so Felix wasn't born at home as planned. Instead I had to give birth at St Mary's Maternity Hospital Kettering, which was a less than happy experience. On my bedside as I recovered – baby taken from me and put in a nursery, just one of the many bits of mismanagement I suffered – was *Small House at Allington* by Anthony Trollope. I had promised to present a session on Trollope's Barchester novels to my National Housewives Register Group – one of the organisations I'd joined in an attempt to get to know people in Wellingborough. At the time of Felix's birth, I was deep in a re-read of all six novels.

When I got home, two days after Felix was born, battered in every sense by St Mary's, my own lovely midwife, who should have done the delivery at home, called. I was still in bed and feeling pretty low. She looked at *Small House at Allington* and said: "Why don't you get something light to read – just for now?" Well, there had been a lot in the papers about a Yorkshire vet named James Herriot so I asked my mother, who was staying with us to sort meals and look after Lucas, to buy me a James Herriot book from the bookshop in town. She came back with his first book and I started to read it. It was the one which opens with an account of Herriot going out in the night to attend to a cow with an everted uterus. Ouch! I was still bleeding and sore from Felix's birth and empathised wincingly with the poor cow and her suffering. When my midwife called later that day, I told her I'd taken her advice but maybe chosen the wrong book for the circumstances.

"Can a human being get an everted uterus?" I asked though gritted teeth.

She twinkled cheerfully back at me and replied: "Only with extreme mismanagement!" Of course, I went on to read all the Herriot books enthusiastically. As a family we later loved the 1980's TV series too and I'm pretty taken with the new version.

Breastfeeding Felix was a different experience. I didn't want Lucas, four years older, to feel left out so I used Felix's daytime feeds as a special time to read to Lucas. I had – and still have – a low, armless Victorian nursing chair given to me by my antique dealer father when I was pregnant with Lucas. I would sit on it with Felix. Lucas would bring the chosen book and perch alongside me. We got through many books during those early months.

One of Lucas's greatest loves was story records. We collected these. The best ones were on EPs and ran about twelve minutes – mostly fairy, traditional or Disney stories. Lucas would choose which one he wanted to hear. I'd put it on the turntable and he'd sit silently in an armchair wearing his father's headphones and following the story in the accompanying book. He'd turn the pages at the right time because there was a signal. "Turn over when

Tinkerbell rings her little bell like this." His focused dedication, aged only three or four, used to amaze visitors and I concluded that concentration is a skill you can deliberately develop. To this day, Lucas is much better at concentrating than I am and I often think that might be related to that early training. We also had LPs of Johnny Morris reading the Thomas the Tank Engine stories, Michael Horden reading Narnia and a lot more.

I promised Lucas that once the new baby arrived we'd have a whole summer at home because I was on maternity leave. The plan was that, while Felix was having his afternoon rest I would teach Lucas to read in advance of his starting school in September. I used the Ladybird series so it was mostly whole word recognition with a bit of phonics thrown in. We used to have fun round the town walking Felix in the pram too. 'Wellingborough' is a good one for whole word recognition because it's a distinctive shape. Moreover, in 1976, almost every car head lamp had the word 'Lucas' on it. By the autumn he was pretty adept at reading and he and I had enjoyed, and both remember, a lot of 'quality time' to get him there.

I did this because education was so slack at the time (one cabinet minister aptly dubbed it 'all happiness and painting') and I was fearful that if I didn't teach him to read then no one else would. As it turned out I was right. He did one year in a primary school in Wellingborough where he was in a large class with a high number of non-English speakers. "Oh I don't need to pay Lucas much attention," his stressed teacher told me. "He can do so much already." I just wished that more had been done to build on the foundations I'd laid. There was no determination (or time or energy?) to move each child forward from his or her starting point.

It was slightly, but only slightly, better once we moved to Kent in 1977. When Lucas was eight, and by then reading fluently, eclectically and independently, a teacher at his primary school asked him what he'd read and he told her he'd just finished *The Hobbit* – which he had. He was quite upset when she accused him of lying. So, I wrote a polite letter to confirm that it was true. Another child, who came to tea with us that day, told me that the teacher had screwed my letter up in annoyance in front of the class. Teachers have a lot to answer for sometimes. I've had many similar conversations with children and thought *Really?* but you could so easily be underestimating the child, so you give him or her the benefit of the doubt. Always.

Felix's route into reading was different. By the time he was three or four I was teaching full-time in Kent and Nick was in charge at home and running Harvest Home Wholefoods. Although we both read to him a lot (even on French campsites) and he had a full-time nursery school place ('The Little Brown Bears') from age three he showed no signs of reading for quite a long time. Then one day Mollie, my mother-in-law, saw him reading a book and expressed surprise. "Oh, I suddenly just seed [sic] how to do it," he informed her nonchalantly.

Felix tells me that he remembers clearly how and when reading clicked. He was almost seven. The book was *My Naughty Little Sister* by Dorothy Edwards. He picked it up, thought it really was about time he got this sorted, looked at the first sentence carefully and realised that he knew what it meant so he studied the next one – and the next. Then he got to the bottom of the page and realised he was reading so he turned the page and carried on... and on.

Children learn to read in all sorts of different ways. It's very individual as I saw with my own children and with the thousands I've worked with professionally. And I contend that no one really understands how it suddenly snaps into focus like muddy water clearing. Felix's elder daughter did it entirely by herself long before she went to school. No one taught her. She had somehow picked it up by some sort of osmosis when she was about three. It's unusual but it happens. No two children are the same.

Learning to read, however you do it, is only the beginning. Everything I've ever experienced or observed in relation to children's reading, my own and other people's, has shown that decoding the squiggles is the easy bit. It's the immersive reading which comes next that really matters. And that's what, I find, that many teachers, then and now, fail to focus on enough. It's why so many young people stop reading when they hit puberty. It's also why – with passion – I wrote *Encouraging Reading* (Bloomsbury 2007) and *Unlocking the Reader in Every Child* (Ransom, new edition 2019). The latter is required reading for TES online literacy courses so perhaps I'm beginning to dent the prevailing attitude. I just wish it were compulsory reading for every teacher everywhere. It might give some parents pause for thought too.

9. THE OPEN UNIVERSITY

Germinal by Emil Zola (1885)

The Open University changed me, and my life, out of all recognition. I loved every minute of the work, including the reading of literally hundreds of books, which led, at last, to me becoming Susan Elkin BA (Hons) in 1988 as opposed to Susan Elkin Cert Ed. I'm afraid, though, that the initial decision to embark on it was born out of less-than-attractive envy and frustration.

I was thirty-four and had been teaching for thirteen years – including two maternity leaves and some part-time work when the boys were very young. But since leaving college I'd only ever actually been out of work for three weeks when we first moved to Wellingborough. By the early 1980s I was working in a girls' school in Sittingbourne teaching up to O Level and having two scale points for extra responsibility (a system long since superseded). I reckon I was doing a reasonable job and, forty years later, a Facebook group for former students in that school now often confirms that I was appreciated, which is good to know. Younger teachers would arrive in the school with their BAs, BScs and PGCEs. They lacked experience and often – frankly – weren't great at the job and were never likely to be. Because, however, they were technically graduates they were paid more than me which was more than infuriating.

One day I flipped and sent for an Open University prospectus. I knew several colleagues (mostly mathematicians) who were already embarked on this. Would it work for me? Of course, rather more positively, I was attracted by the prospect of studying more English – like the fondly remembered English course at Bishop Otter. And strangely enough, a few years later, I found Mr Townsend again. Long since retired from Bishop Otter, he was now working part-time for the Open University and I attended a couple of sessions he ran at a Saturday face-to-face day. So there was actually a link.

I was blown away by the Open University arts prospectus. Imagine studying eleven 19th century novels and five early 20th century ones. Or eight Shakespeare plays. It sounded like paradise to me. I really did want to do this but, bearing in mind that I had a full-time teaching job, children aged ten and six and involvement in Harvest Home Wholefoods, it was going to take some planning and thinking about.

Somehow I would need to find fifteen or so hours a week from February to October for the next several years. And I needed to get Nick onside – which wasn't difficult. At the beginning I don't think he really understood why I was so desperate to do it but he always supported unfailingly anything I decided to do. Some years I would have to go to summer school for a week. There would be occasional Saturday classes and tutorials. Nick agreed that he could, and would, hold the fort while I did all this.

Another factor was that Open University fees in 1982 were still pretty modest. Moreover, Kent County Council, my employer before schools managed their own budgets, had a policy of part-funding any teacher studying in search of better qualifications including the Open University and summer school fees. In cash terms it therefore wasn't going to cost me much but the time would need to be carefully managed.

I applied and was happy to be offered a place. Not that the Open University is competitive. It's open. That's the whole point. There are no entry qualifications or other barriers but it could have been oversubscribed. It was an exhilarating moment, though. Yes, I really was going to do this, starting in February 1982. And I was going to apply myself to it fully so that I would acquit myself as well as I possibly could. This was my chance to offset all my previous educational shortcomings and gaps.

The Open University works completely differently now but when I enrolled you couldn't do a degree in English alone. It had to be general arts so that's what I did, choosing as many English options as I could as I went along. It operated on a credit system which you built up by taking whole or half credits courses which were pitched at different levels. You could do these in any order you liked but you had to do a foundation course first. Eventually, long after my time, the Open University came into line with other universities and the usual 360 credits arrangement. I got some remission for my Cert Ed and needed five and a half Open University credits for a full honours degree which I spent six years getting.

Towards the end of 1981 I was invited to a meeting at Christ Church College, Canterbury, with other imminent beginners to meet my tutor, Anne Stott, who was, and is, a historian. She tutored two of the courses I did and was to remain my personal tutor for the next six years. Spouses and partners were invited to that meeting so Nick was able to get the flavour of where I was going. Anne, now Doctor Anne Stott, has published several fine historical biographies since then. I have reviewed her books for newspapers and magazines and am still in touch with her.

Thus, in 1982 I began the Arts Foundation course which started with writing technique and study skills before embarking on a detailed, multidisciplinary study of arts in the 19th century: Jane Eyre, music hall songs, John Stewart Mill, Pre-Raphaelites, Mahew, Ruskin, Mendelssohn and the like. Doors began to burst open. *A Midsummer Night's Dream* was also in the mix but I can't remember how that fitted into the pattern.

The first batch of course materials arrived in mid-January although the start date was a month later. It felt better than Christmas and my birthday rolled into one – and always did for the next six years each and every time one of those parcels arrived. By then I'd claimed a corner of the spare bedroom and put a table in the window – my Open University desk. Why should I wait a month? Before that day was out I was off like a marathon runner at the starting point. I reached for the notebooks I'd bought and the first page of the coursework book, which guided you step by step, and got going. I'm sure the equivalent now, forty years later, would all be online.

I reached the end of the first mini-module before the course had officially started so of course I immediately wrote the first assignment. On a full credit course there were usually eight of these, about one a month, and together they constituted 50% of the final mark for that course. The other 50% depended on a formal exam. A college hall in Chatham was the local Open University exam centre and I sat seven three-hour papers there between 1982 and 1987. The college and the hall are long gone. There's a housing estate on the site now.

Timing was everything. Because I started the course a month early I remained ahead for the rest of the year. That meant, for example, that I could take a week out when my grandmother came to stay for a few days at Easter or when my school friend came over from Italy in August. It also gave me some extra revision time in hand at the end of the course before the exam. It worked so well that I made this my working method throughout my degree. I completely ignored the dates on blocks of work. I was always at least a month ahead, thereby sparing myself the fear and stress of ever falling behind. There were timed supporting radio and TV programmes with which I was always out of synch but I soon discovered I could get them free, direct from Milton Keynes on cassette (remember those?) or video, so I did.

Single-mindedness was what found me the time. I jettisoned everything except teaching, which had to include a bit of private coaching because there was never enough money. I needed two hours each evening usually from about 7.30–9.30pm and four hours or so each Saturday and Sunday: a total of eighteen hours per week. I gave up the choral society I'd been singing in and made it clear to everyone that I was simply not available to socialise on weekday evenings although of course there were occasional parents' evenings at school which I had to attend. I'd race home from school, get any marking and preparation done (or get up very early the next morning and do it), make everyone's packed lunch, get dinner on the table and then bolt off to my spare room desk while Nick cleared up and got the children to bed. We were a good team. That was the routine for nine months of the year, for six years. Harvest Home Wholefoods was dwindling by then, although I have a vivid memory of listening over and over to *The Marriage of Figaro* to familiarise myself with it while I was making dozens of cheese scones and that must have been in my second Open University year when the course I'd chosen was The Enlightenment (*Tom Jones*, which I'd read at college, Hume, Adam Smith, Mozart and a lot more).

School holidays – Easter, summer and the May half term – were a bonus. I could then get my two hours done in the morning and keep afternoons and evenings free to spend with the children. Or I could do four hours in the day and give myself the next day off. It worked as long as I was strictly self-disciplined. The children, incidentally, were remarkably understanding considering how young they were. They were very good about allowing me the space I needed. Nick was always around and he trained them not to disturb me other than in a dire emergency.

I used to take them to places too. When we camped (very low budget holiday) outside Paris in 1983 we went to the Panthéon where Voltaire and Rousseau are buried because it was relevant to my Enlightenment course. Zola is in there too but I hadn't quite got to him at that point. We also took the boys to the Louvre where Nick showed them the Mona Lisa and Venus de Milo while I went to the top floor to make notes on the Chardin paintings for an essay I had to write that autumn. As soon as we got home Lucas, then twelve, and I went to the Wallace Collection so that I could study the Bouchers for the same essay. In 1985 we were on holiday in Dorset and I was frantically gathering information about the architecture of Kingston Lacey, built in the 1660s just after the Restoration which was relevant to the 17th century course I was doing that year. I hoped that in a sense my Open University degree was widening their horizons too and I think it did. "We're going to one of Mummy's Open University places," they'd say cheerfully. Today, they both now look back on those visits with affection so I clearly wasn't traumatising them.

For me it was real, internalised, integrated learning which stuck as opposed to the detached memorising which I could never manage satisfactorily at school. Moreover, I tried to apply everything I was learning wherever I was. I remember, for instance, being thrilled to notice for the first time that in the parish church at Tunstall, which we often visited on walks out from Sittingbourne, you can see a broken stone in the wall where the rood screen was removed in the 1640s – exactly what I was studying in my 17th century course in 1985. Rood screens were perceived as divisive. Parliamentarian factions believed that priests should be in the same space as the congregation just as they wanted barriers between royalty and the populace lowered. Many of those screens were destroyed by troops or expediently taken down by parishes. And there it all was over four hundred years later – in a little church, a mile from home that I passed several times a week and often went to concerts in.

I also had a policy of studying the examples given in the course materials, which were effectively the equivalent of lectures and tutorials in a conventional university, and the associated reading and then finding my own. There was a perception among some Open University students that 'they' didn't want you to stray outside the course in your essays. I decided that must be nonsense. It didn't feel like real learning if you simply regurgitated what 'they' said. You surely had to make it your own? So I made a practice of taking the information and applying it to something else. Lady Bankes, a Royalist who bravely held out at Corfe Castle in Dorset for three years before the besieged castle was finally destroyed by Parliamentarian forces in 1645, was a good example. She wasn't mentioned in the course notes but her story illustrated lots of points in one of my essays.

When I was doing the Arts Foundation Course in 1982 there was a production of *A Midsummer Night's Dream* (which by then, I'd taught and seen several times) at the National Theatre. Directed by Bill Bryden and starring Robert Stephens and Susan Fleetwood it was played without interval and had attracted a lot of critical acclaim. I needed to see this, I thought. So I went to a Saturday matinee on my own which was affordable in a way that a family trip for four wouldn't have been. Weeks later at Summer School (Warwick University) one of the tutors asked if any of us had seen it so obviously I piped up – the only one in the room. After the session one of the other students asked me incredulously how I'd managed to see it. I simply didn't know how to answer. "I bought a ticket and went" sounded a bit rude. It was an example, though, of my proactively surrounding myself with the subject matter of the course while other students passively did what they were told and no more. I got the impression that many were simply nervous of thinking for themselves, or round the subject, which I found puzzling.

It's why, of course, the learning stuck. I didn't need to memorise the details. I could look up anything which needed to be checked. But I developed a real grasp of the issues and it taught me a lot about different ways in which people learn which was useful for the day job.

The other way in which I tried to keep ahead was by anticipating which courses I intended to do later and preparing for them over a long trajectory. I planned to do the Shakespeare course eventually and knew which plays were coming up so I made a point of catching any production I could of those plays, as I spotted them, especially the ones I hadn't seen before.

And my eye was firmly fixed on the 19th century novel course which I decided I'd do in my third year. The novels were listed in the prospectus. Obviously, as I'd been an English specialist for years, I'd read a number of them before but as soon as I'd made the decision to do an Open University degree, I began reading or re-reading each one of them systematically. Thus, when I arrived at the beginning of my third year I'd already read all sixteen novels, which included some French and Russian titles in translation, at least once. By the time I actually started that course I was busily reading them again. I read most of them at least three times before the final exam. And I did this by not reading anything which wasn't connected with the course from February to October. I would make a list on my pin board of other books I was saving for the three-month Open University break from October to February.

My first encounter with *Germinal* was startling. Because I hadn't previously read any 19th century French literature I was astonished by how explicit it is compared with British novels dating from the same period. The account of Maheu being washed by his wife when he comes home covered in coal dust from the mine is both graphic and erotic. When the Maheus want to make love they disappear and the children know they're expected to keep out of the way. It's matter-of-fact and casual. The poverty and the strike are moving because of course this is a coal mining novel – like much of DH Lawrence and Richard Llewellyn's *How Green Was My Valley*. But it was the suspense which really got under my skin. Of course there's a climactic pit disaster and, the first time I read it, it kept me awake frantically turning the pages until 2.00am (on a school night!) because I simply had to find out whether they get out of the flooded mine. It was some of the most arresting fiction I'd ever read, and it still hits me between the eyes when I re-read it today although, obviously, I know the outcome now.

The rest of that course included, in no particular order, *Mansfield Park, Madame Bovary, Middlemarch, Wuthering Heights, Anna Karenina* and *Tess of the D'Urbervilles* plus early 20th century titles such as *Mrs Dalloway, Portrait of the Artist as a Young Man* and *Heart of Darkness*. I had a wonderful cassette of Paul Schofield reading the latter which I found in a second-hand shop. I played it over and over and still connect the text with his inimitable, rich chocolatey voice.

I wrote my eight essays and got average marks although the tutor, who taught at University of Kent, clearly had a very specific feminist agenda of her own and we often didn't see eye to eye which seemed to be depressing my marks. I was therefore utterly astonished – and delighted – to get a distinction for the course overall. I must have done an exceptionally good final exam to offset the coursework marks although at that point they didn't give you the actual marks as they did by the time I was in my final year. It was by far the best Christmas present I had that year. And of course, aged thirty-eight, the first thing I did was to ring my mother to tell her, as if I were twelve again and running home from school to share good news.

Naturally there was a knock-on effect in terms of confidence and determination. I could actually do this! There was no grade for the Arts Foundation course apart from pass or fail and I'd got a two (the grading was Distinction, two, three, four, fail) for the

Enlightenment the year before. I was actually, for the first time in my life, excelling. And it was very exciting.

After the 17th century (Hobbes, Bunyan, John Donne, Civil War, Purcell and lots more) in 1985 I took just a half credit, Shakespeare, which I loved, as detailed in Chapter 4. By then I was getting top marks for each course. I needed a little more time that year – hence the half credit – because I wanted to try my hand at O Level exam marking which bit several weeks out in the summer. I hated it and never did it again.

So I was now at four and a half credits and needed one more full credit or two halves. In my final year, 1987, I took The Romantic Poets (Keats, Blake, Wordsworth, Coleridge, Byron and Shelley) which was a half credit. I found Shelley so difficult that I worked at him relentlessly and ended up choosing not one, but two Shelley questions in the final exam which amused me at the time. They were giving us proper percentage marks by then. When the course result came through, I got 93% – not bad for someone who got a low O Level English Literature grade and didn't do English A Level.

Much less successful was the final half credit I did alongside the poets. I'd run out of arts courses and was beginning to think about looking for promotion in teaching. Surely it would be useful if I did something on education? So, I did a half credit in Education Management which was a mistake. I've always loathed education theory. I suppose it has its place but it isn't for me. I did my best with the jargon and the case studies, but it wasn't great. I got a level three pass. I can't remember the percentage but it must have been 55% or thereabouts – the lowest I ever got in my whole degree.

The upshot of all this was that in December 1997 I got the confirmation that I had achieved a First Class Honours degree. Of course I was expecting that. I had studied the Open University's published tables very carefully and could see that my marks, despite Education Management, put me pretty near the top of the first class section of the grid. Nonetheless it was extraordinary to see it in writing. It was one in the eye for lots of people, including – oddly – Nick who had said more than once during the six years that he couldn't see me achieving more than an average degree. I teased him about that for the rest of his life and in the end he admitted that he had underestimated me. "I now know that you can do anything you set your mind too," he once told me fondly. Our story was definitely not *Educating Rita* in which the husband is so jealous that he burns her books.

I was due to graduate at the Brighton Centre in April 1988 but before that something terrifying happened and I found myself doing a great deal of a very different sort of reading.

Just after Christmas my father, sixty-six, collapsed with a mysterious illness. He was the fittest man any of us knew. I remember him catching flu (from me when I first started teaching and was still living at home) and having a couple of days in bed in 1968 but apart from that I don't think he'd ever had a day off sick. Now, suddenly, he couldn't stand or hold his head up. Normally he drove out to antiques fairs or to buy antiques every day as well as leading his folk dance band, The Southerners. He and my mother had sold the shop in 1976 and gone to live in a south Kent village but they were both still active and working. She rang me in a state of petrified panic and I got in the car and went to them immediately. I did what I could in terms of comfort and common sense. She didn't really know what to do and neither did I. The next day there was a call to me at school to tell me that she'd called an ambulance and he'd been admitted to a hospital in Dover. So I went straight there after school.

He'd been diagnosed with Guillain Barré syndrome, a condition originally identified by two early 20th century French doctors. It's supposed to be a rare condition but I have heard of lots of cases since 1998. It affects the nerves and no one knows what causes it. In my father's case it caused complete organ failure and by the second day in hospital he was in Intensive Care with all body functions, including breathing, being supported artificially. It was utterly terrifying.

Soon they transferred him to St Thomas' Hospital in London in an intensive care ambulance. The truth was – and probably still is – that no one knows what causes this dreadful condition and the medics have no strategy for dealing with it. I spent hours at his bedside in intensive care feeling helpless, and lost in admiration for the calm, skilled staff. They were so good at what they did. All I knew about was old poems and what use is that in such circumstances? My mother, meanwhile, had almost fallen apart.

Of course, I read everything I could lay hands on to find out more about GBS. Joseph Heller of *Catch-22* fame, for instance, had had GBS and wrote a memoir about it entitled *No Laughing Matter* (1986). The hospitals pointed us towards local networks but it was quite difficult to access information quickly in those pre-Google days. Another famous sufferer was Tony Wedgwood Benn, former Labour cabinet minister and courter of controversy. He supportively phoned my mother to commiserate one evening. Whatever you think about some of the things he did and said he was evidently a very kind man.

They told us that eventually the condition would probably reverse itself. It was usually just a matter of patience although they wouldn't be drawn on what the after-effects might be. That was hard to hang on to during the many weeks that Father lay, sedated but trying to communicate in blinks, in intensive care. After a couple of weeks at St Thomas' he was moved back to William Harvey Hospital in Ashford, Kent. It was mid-March before we got a shred of good news. A physio said she'd detected a whisper on his lungs. He was beginning to breathe again. And so could the rest of us.

He was finally discharged from hospital at the end of March. My graduation ceremony was mid-April. Although I had, for years, set my heart on my parents being there, I had more or less accepted that it wasn't going to happen. His recovery, though, was almost as extraordinary as the decline into GBS nearly three months earlier. Once we'd talked him out of the sedation-induced delusions he picked up rapidly.

In the end, on graduation day my mother found the strength to drive him in his big car (Nissan Prairie) to Rottingdean from south Kent, although she wouldn't normally touch it and only drove her small runabout. We met them there and had lunch. Then, leaving our own car at Rottingdean, Nick drove the Prairie into Brighton with us all on board so that he could drop us at the Brighton Centre entrance and then park. Both my parents were thus in the hall, against all the odds, to see me in my dark blue academic gown, one of the very first across the platform. And I insisted on having a group photograph afterwards rather than the usual formal portrait of me with scroll. I was almost as thrilled, under the circumstances, to have my dad there as I was to have got the degree. That photograph still hangs in pride of place in my dining room.

It wasn't a long-term happy ending for Father's health though. Although he was, almost unbelievably, driving his car and caravan round the Dordogne with my sister and her children in summer 1987 the recovery didn't last. Eighteen months later he went down with GBS again and that really isn't supposed to happen. This time he was taken to Guy's Hospital, where he lay for three weeks, although he never needed intensive care again.

The medics, led by the newly ennobled Ian McColl who took a personal interest because the case was now very unusual indeed, were baffled. In the end they suggested trying very high dosage steroids which the patient readily agreed to because he just wanted to get better and would have consented to anything. So he went home with the pills and within two or three years had developed kidney failure, probably caused by the steroids. He died in 1997 after several increasingly miserable years of dialysis and failing health. So, indirectly, GBS killed him in the end.

10. MUSIC

Observers Book of Music by Freda Dinn (1953)

I suppose I've always been musical. I could, for example, pick out a nursery rhyme with one finger on the piano before I went to school without understanding what I was doing or how I was doing it. Not that ever I took to the piano. It was just the instrument which was there. Each of my grandmothers had one in her 'best' room, although neither played. It was simply what their generation did. Aunty June, who must have had some lessons in her own childhood, taught me to play a few scales with the correct fingers but that was about as far as it went.

My earliest memory of making music with others is of singing in the infants school choir at Rathfern Road School. It must have been a selected group because it wasn't a whole class. I have no idea whether we were picked (maybe – I could certainly sing in tune) or whether we signed up for it, so to speak. What I do remember with great clarity is doing 'Cockles and Mussels'. "You have to sing this verse quietly because she's died," said the teacher. I had no idea what she was talking about because I didn't understand a single word of the song. I liked the tune, though, and there was something about performing in a group which appealed.

When I was seven and had progressed across the playground to the junior school, we could often hear recorders, violins or cellos being played in the hall off which most of the classrooms opened. One day someone came into our classroom and said: "Does anyone want to play the violin? If so, bring a note tomorrow."

Hand up, note brought and I was off. It seemed a good idea to me because I knew that my father had played violin when he was a boy. He often told us how he'd played in the Crystal Palace, which must have been in the early 1930s because it burned down in 1936. He'd have been ten or eleven and presumably part of some sort of school or regional group. He left school at sixteen, went to work in an estate agent's office and enlisted in the RAF at eighteen. When I went home and asked for my permission note to start, he hadn't played for many years although I knew there was still an old violin in a wooden case in my grandparents' attic.

He, and everyone else in the family, was enthusiastic about my having a go. My very elderly great grandmother, skilled in needlework, was commissioned to make me a little velvet pad with a ribbon strap which was what children then used in lieu of a shoulder rest. It was navy blue. The school lent me a violin. My grandparents bought me a music case with my initials on.

Each week a little group of about eight of us were called out of the classroom for our violin lesson. We stood in a semicircle around our teacher, Mrs Clements, who sat mostly at the piano. We were taught the vocabulary of violin anatomy: tail piece, pegs, finger board, f hole, sound post and how to erect and fold up a music stand. The latter may sound trivial but it's a vital life skill for any musician. More importantly we learned the names of the strings, how to hold the instrument and the bow, how to create notes with fingers and what those notes looked like – in length and pitch – on a musical stave. Gradually I learned to play simple tunes and to read music. Then the school started a rudimentary orchestra with cellos, recorders and piano. It met after school on

Fridays and I really liked that. I still have very tatty copies of one or two of the pieces, often by Adam Carse, that we played. Carse was a composer and arranger whose music for young players was far reaching. He lived from 1878 to 1958 so I now realise he must have been still alive when I first met his pieces. 'Carmen's Whistle' sticks in my mind because I thought the title was funny.

By the time I left junior school I had my own violin which had, no doubt, 'come into the shop'. I was probably at about Grade 1 to 2 although there was no suggestion of anyone taking exams at Rathfern. I was never going to be a great player but I liked doing it. I often wonder how many of the rest of that class went on playing or maybe still play.

Meanwhile we had a very good music teacher at primary school, Mr Oliver James, who taught singing to all classes as well as having a class of his own. I joined his choir and we took part, more than once, in a local primary school singing festival – going to a different school for rehearsals with other schools – and then finally performing at Catford Broadway Theatre which everyone in those days referred to as 'the Town Hall' because it was part of the same complex.

Another Rathfern teacher, Mr Glynn Harris, was hot on radio technology and later went to work in BBC schools broadcasting. While he was with us he made intra-school radio programmes with the children in his class and broadcast them to the rest of us in our classrooms. More importantly, as far I was concerned, he would play us pieces on the record player in assembly and talk about them. I was so excited by Ronald Binge's *Elizabethan Serenade* (1951) that my parents bought me a record of it. It was also through Mr Harris that, among other pieces, I first heard and got familiar with *The Carnival of Animals*.

At the same time there was a lot of music at home. In 1952, when I was five, my father was still teaching maths and PE at Addey and Stanhope's School in Deptford while my mother ran the shop.

His school put on a production of *The Mikado* for which my father did front of house. Gilbert and Sullivan was completely new to him although my mother was familiar with it because her granny had loved it and would sing her the songs. I was taken to Addey and Stanhope's to watch *The Mikado* which I think was my first experience of live theatre. I was instantly bitten by the Gilbert and Sullivan bug, almost as much as my father now was. He took me backstage at the end and Petti-Sing gave me her fan so perhaps it was the final performance. Soon our house was full of Gilbert and Sullivan LPs that were played over and over again on the radiogram, which was purchased as soon as the family business began to pick up. And I was embarked on a life-long passion for Gilbert and Sullivan. I know every note and many of the words and have seen, literally, hundreds of performances over the years. These days, moreover, it would be an unusual year if I didn't review at least three or four Gilbert and Sullivan shows, of which more in Chapter 12.

There was other music too. As my parents got better off they took to going occasionally to the theatre. If he'd liked the show, Father usually bought the LP afterwards so the house was so full of, for instance, the sounds of *Rigoletto*, *La Traviata*, *Salad Days*, *Il Trovatore*, *Carmen*, *My Fair Lady*, *The Student Prince* and Flanders and Swan that it was almost as if I'd seen the shows myself. The music simply soaked itself into my head. Derek McCulloch's Saturday morning *Children's Favourites* taught me a lot too. It was there that I first heard most of the 'classical' pot-boilers: favourites such as *The Dance of the Sugar Plum Fairy*, *The Moonlight Sonata* and *The March* from *Aida*.

When I was about eight or nine someone gave me *The Observer's Book of Music* as a birthday or Christmas present. I read this neat little book a lot and can remember its contents very clearly – the beginning of my wider musical education, I suppose.

Acquiring Observer's books was quite a thing for 1950's children and when I married Nick in 1969 we merged our collections and discarded the duplications. He didn't have the music one so we kept mine, first published in 1953. Although I had it for many years my original copy is now unaccountably lost. Happily, I spotted a similar one recently in Ely market. So I bought it for £6 which made me chuckle since the original 1950's price was 5/- or 25p.

And, golly, how I've enjoyed the nostalgic revisit. It packs in a deal of information but is never patronising. I struggle, even now, to understand the opening section 'Sound and how we hear it' which is pure physics but, as ever, I really like the detailed account of musical instruments and how they work. There's a drawing of Beethoven's pianoforte, an account of the evolution of the cornet, a wonderful drawing of a Russian bassoon along with details about stringed instruments and not, obviously, just the four you find in a standard symphony orchestra. For such a small book, the amount of information Freda Dinn squeezes in is extraordinary.

She's good on terms in common use too. I think this was probably where I first read, for example, that *scherzo* is the Italian for joke so it usually denotes a jokey sort of movement in a symphony and that *andante* means walking pace. The little pieces we were playing at primary school didn't, in general, use these grown-up terms much. Then of course, a year or two later when I started first French and then Latin at secondary school, the linguistic links began to make sense.

The Observer's Book of Music ends with biographical notes on composers. The criteria for inclusion seem quaint now. Several contemporary composers are in: Britten, Arnold, Bax, Barber, Walton etc. Of course all the obvious greats are there: Beethoven, Tchaikovsky, Brahms, Purcell and the like but some of her choices, such as Cui and Palmgren, seem a bit obscure in the 21st century. She includes Samuel Coleridge-Taylor and Ethel Smythe – the former the only black entry and the latter the only woman – and this was why I grew up having heard of both of them although it took the world most of my lifetime to wake up to the fact that, of course, neither was unique. Paul Sharp provides a nice little pencil sketch of each composer.

Rediscovering this book was fun. I realise now that the whole of the 'Observer's' series comprised beginner's guides. They were child-friendly but not intended exclusively for children. Indeed, even now, anyone wanting to learn more about music – mostly, but not entirely, classical – could do a lot worse than start here. It's widely available on second-hand book websites.

The music in my home when I was growing up was live as well as recorded. In about 1954 my mother joined a folk dance evening class and could see that it really needed live music. She got friendly with the class tutor (who became a life-long friend to both my parents) and together, at about the same time that I started playing, they persuaded my father to get his violin out and start practising. Night after night, when I'd been put to bed, I could hear him downstairs playing 'The Irish Washerwoman', 'Cock of the North' and lots of other jigs and reels. He'd signed up for refresher lessons with the same teacher who had taught him in boyhood. Before long he was playing with an accordionist for children's dancing and by the early 1960s he was leading his own band, The Southerners. They played for dances in many venues, took part in festivals all over Europe, travelled to the USA, did some work for the BBC and made lots of recordings. In the end he had to join the Musician's Union because he was semi-professional although of course there was still the antiques business to run at the same time. So one way and another our home was pretty musical although, apart from the handful of big operas that my father loved, no one was very interested in the classical stuff I was rapidly becoming engrossed by.

In 1958, when I progressed to Sydenham High School, I wanted to continue with my violin. Individual music lessons were a chargeable extra but fortunately in my case this wasn't a barrier and my father happily coughed up for the next seven years. By then I'd had three years of free lessons and a pretty good start. Today, of course, this would be very unlikely and that's an educational disaster. My primary school contemporaries came from a wide range of backgrounds and the opportunity was freely and casually there for any child who fancied having a go. Another half dozen in my class did cello with Mr Ticciati on the same basis and there was a recorder group along with the singing that everyone did. Today the ever-worsening attitude to the arts, the relentless focus on STEM (science, technology, engineering, maths) and the chilly testing regime, means that the arts in general and music in particular really are becoming elitist subjects: if you can't pay you can't have it. This is a personal tragedy for every child who is the victim of arts-deprived education and, more widely, for the future of arts organisations.

But, thank goodness, I was one of the lucky ones. At Sydenham High School I had a weekly violin lesson with Miss Oglethorpe, played every Wednesday in the junior orchestra and sang in the junior choir almost from my first week. It's a good job, with hindsight, that I was as committed to the violin as I was. Because I was a mere first year, I got the short straw. The school had a half day on a Friday (bliss!) but my violin lesson was timetabled for 4.00pm on Friday afternoon. You were supposed to have a school dinner and then go to a classroom with others to do your prep (homework) under the supervision of a prefect until it was time for whatever commitment you'd stayed for. Well I loathed, detested and dreaded school dinners (much compulsion to eat some of the most dreadful food I've seen anywhere) and I certainly wasn't going to succumb to a fifth one in the week if I could possibly avoid it. So I would leave with everyone else at 12.50pm and go to the Sydenham shop, the other branch of the family business. There my grandmother would give me a really nice lunch, after which I'd sit in the back room and do my weekend prep. At the right time my grandfather (one of the kindest men I've ever met) would drive me back to school for my violin lesson. Usually he would also wait for me and drive me home so that I didn't have to get the bus.

At the end of my first term at Sydenham I went to the senior school concert. I went alone so I suppose it was before I'd made friends. I must, I now realise, have been more single-minded than most eleven year olds to do that by myself simply because I was interested. That year there was an unusually talented group of Upper Sixth musicians and they played the first movement of the 'Brandenburg Concerto number five' which, of course, I'd neither heard before nor heard of, although I'd probably read about JS Bach in *The Observer's Book of Music*. I knew nothing about suspensions or modulations and I barely knew what a key change is. But I sat, transfixed on the edge of my seat, during that fantastic long harpsichord solo (played on piano in this performance) listening to Bach magically winding and winding back to the statement, full orchestra tune which I knew, by instinct, would bounce back at the end of the solo. I was exhilarated, thrilled and instantly, permanently in love with the piece.

So I tried to find it again afterwards but failed. We didn't have Google in 1958. I had no idea there were six of these concertos. I didn't ask at home because I knew that neither of my parents knew anything about classical music, which was silly because, had he known how interested I was, my father would have taken the trouble to find out. Or I could have asked at school. But I didn't. Wind forward five years and I'm at Royal Festival Hall with one of my many male friends – he'd got comps for the Stuttgart Chamber Orchestra through the music club at his college. We heard three Brandenburg concerti including number five. Suddenly – there it was in all its glory and I was, again, on the edge of my seat and utterly delighted to have 'found' it. After that I bought a record. The wonder of that extraordinary harpsichord solo stops me in my tracks to this day if, for example, I catch it on Radio 3. And recently, for the first time ever, over sixty years since I first heard it, I played the second violin part in a music workshop: unadulterated joy!

By the time I was fourteen I had taken and passed Grade 5 (with merit – hurrah) and was invited to transfer from the junior to the senior orchestra which, among other duties, accompanied the hymns in assembly on Thursdays. Miss Barbara Strudwick was now my violin teacher and she also directed the orchestra. At the first rehearsal I attended they were having a stab at Schubert's symphony number eight 'The Unfinished' which was quite a learning curve because there were several bits of notation in the grown-up Breitkopf and Härtel part I was given, that I'd never seen before. The piece grabbed me, though, and I borrowed a recording from Lewisham library and played it over and over. By that time I had a record player in my bedroom.

I also started reading little biographies of composers from the school library: Schubert, Haydn, Handel, Beethoven and more. Who were these people and what led them to compose this marvellous stuff? I was hungry for information.

As I progressed through school I was involved in pretty much every musical activity going. For example I sang (as a Gossip) in a production of Britten's *Noye's Fludde*. There was a *Messiah* (Handel) in which I played in the orchestra and a *Christmas Oratorio* (Bach) in which I was one of several girls who emerged from the orchestra to sing a bit of recitative. Most memorable of all was an inter-school performance of *The Creation* (Haydn) at Caxton Hall which was conducted by Sir David Willcocks.

The rule is that you can't take practical music exams above Grade 5 unless you have passed Grade 5 theory. There was no pressure so for a while I rejected this route – I'd just play. There was plenty going on, after all. I used to play with my father's band if they were short and I was nearly always welcome to sit in. I taught myself to play accompaniment guitar so that I could sing solo folk songs too.

When one of the dance demonstration groups my parents were involved with was invited to be the cabaret entertainment at the Buckingham Palace Staff Christmas Ball, with most of the Royal Family in attendance, I sang the beautiful Klezmer song 'Donna Donna', solo, which was quite an experience.

After a bit, I changed my mind and did the dreaded Grade 5 theory. I was much better at Italian terms – I'm a words person – than I ever was at the mathematical side of music or worse, things such as the mechanics of harmony. Fortunately, there was always a choice of question. In the end I passed the theory exam and scraped through both Violin Grade 7 and 8 before I left school.

Once at college I did a lot of my solo folk singing but less on the violin, although I have fond memories of accompanying the slow movement of Mozart's Clarinet Concerto at a college concert and there was a production of *Noye's Fludde* (again) in the Chapel for which I played second violin in the string quartet. I also took part, with my father, in the English Folk Dance and Song Society's annual all-weekend festival at the Royal Albert Hall each February.

After Nick and I were married and my teaching job was beginning to settle down, I joined the Lewisham Philharmonic Orchestra and we played several concerts at the Broadway Theatre in Catford (a familiar venue for many years by now – all our School Speech days were held there). One such concert was 'Tchaikovsky's First Piano Concerto' with Peter Katin as soloist. The orchestra standard was pretty low and there were a lot of parts missing so in my first term with them I was puzzled about how we were ever going to stage a concert and charge people to come in. I knew nothing about stiffeners and deps – the people who, for a fee, help out on the day. Almost all community orchestras rely on this to some extent. In Lewisham Philharmonic's case the solution was the Royal Artillery from nearby Woolwich. They rode in at the last minute like the cavalry in an old Western – making the end result actually sound quite decent.

The move to Wellingborough meant that I had to find another orchestra and I played violin two with Kettering Symphony Orchestra for four years. I ended up as treasurer of KSO because they were desperate. I am utterly hopeless with figures and money but agreed under pressure to take it on, knowing that help was available at home. Nick did the accounts very competently which I would then present at the AGM hoping, praying almost, that no one would ask a question and thank goodness they didn't.

During those years at Lewisham and Kettering I learned lots of new pieces. I discovered 'Dvorak 8' which I played with both orchestras and which has been my favourite symphony ever since. I accompanied all the major piano concertos at Kettering along with lots of overtures, marches and symphonies. Mollie, my mother-in-law, who came with George and Nick to most of the Kettering concerts, bought me Yehudi Menhuin's autobiography *Unfinished Journey* in 1976 when it was first published – books were still firmly in the musical mix.

It fell apart, gradually, though once we moved to Kent in 1977. I was teaching full-time and terrifically busy. Moreover, Lucas had started violin and was doing well. He overtook me so fast (although I helped him a lot at the very start) that I got a bit disheartened. Gradually I became a lapsed violinist although I sang for many years in Sittingbourne Orpheus Choral Society so I was still reading and making music – *Messiah*, *The Creation*, *Elijah*, *St John Passion* and lots more. When I read Vikram Seth's novel *An Equal Music* in 2004, I thought ruefully: *Yes, I understand this very well. I used to play the violin.*

Then, in January 2014, came an epiphany. We were beginning to think about downsizing from out great barn of a house in Sittingbourne and I was turning out cupboards. When I found my violin, I sat back on my haunches and asked myself: "Well what am I going to do with this, then? Sell it?" No! suddenly I was assailed by an overwhelming urge to play it, partly because my sister, whose violin journey was similar to mine, had begun playing again. I took the instrument that I'd had since I was about fourteen to a luthier and had it restored to playing standard. He also re-haired my bow and advised me to ditch my old case which was infested by (invisible) weevils who had eaten most of the bow hair.

Then I got out all the old folk tune books. The melodies are very simple but perfect for getting your fingers moving and honing your intonation when you're long, very long, out of practice. After a while I had some lessons locally and I joined the 'returners' orchestra in Ashford where my sister played. At the first rehearsal I went to they were doing the opening movement of Beethoven's 'First Piano Concerto' with their very talented director on piano. Of course I knew every note of how it goes. By then I had over half a century of concert going and listening to recordings behind me. But suddenly here I was playing in the orchestra. I was so thrilled that at the end I cried. I hadn't dreamed I'd ever take part in anything like that again however low the standard of my effort. In October 2014 I went very nervously, with my sister, to Benslow Music in Hertfordshire for a four-day strings course. On the morning of the fourth day I managed to sight read all the way through the second violin part of an early Mozart quartet and, although I played it badly, I held my own right to the last bar. The satisfaction was better than every drug in the world.

In the last ten years I have been to Benslow dozens more times. I've played lots of concerts at Ashford because I continued, until recently, to drive back from London into Kent to take part. I've now been playing with Hayes Symphony Orchestra, local to my home in London, for seven years. My sister and I have started a just-for-pleasure string quartet which meets for an all day session in her house once every six weeks or so. I attend workshops in Folkestone, Canterbury and London and play duets with friends and family as often as possible. I do an annual music summer school each August. And I adore every note of it.

There are other aspects to all this too. Inevitably, since I review performing arts events professionally, work and my main non-work activity have often blurred in recent years. Classical music concert reviews have gradually become part of my professional mix.

Moreover, amateur music making is like church. It's a fine way of getting to know like-minded, supportive people. It's a network. I might go to a two-day course at, say, City Lit in London to learn a work and see several people I know – from Benslow, or Folkestone or somewhere none of us can remember. Players at Hayes Symphony Orchestra have become friends as have some of the people I play with elsewhere. Yes, to have been born musical, is a bonus in many ways – and reading music is just another form of reading.

And I'm glad a friend introduced me to the novels of Isabel Rogers about the Stockwell Park Orchestra. They are wittily entertaining. She's a cellist who knows, really knows, the sort of people who play together for pleasure and what makes them tick. I feel I know every character.

11. CHRISTINA

Christina Rossetti Selected Poems Ed CH Sisson (1984)

I'm in the Round Room at the old British Library in Bloomsbury, surrounded by dusty, quiet history and arc-shaped bookcases. The ghosts of Bernard Shaw, Charles Darwin and Virginia Woolf, among others, are hovering and looking over my shoulder. In front of me, at my leather-topped, brass-studded desk for the day, is a book, which I've ordered and the fetchers have placed here for me: *Goblin Market and Other Poems* by Christina Rossetti. It was published in 1862 and that's the date stamped at the front by the British Library, when it was catalogued.

The pages are uncut. And I'm spellbound. It means that whichever Macmillan was in charge of the family business at that point, deposited this book here on publication as required by law. He would have placed one in each of the UK's other five copyright or 'legal deposit' libraries too: The Bodliean Libraries, University of Oxford; Cambridge University Library; National Library of Scotland, Edinburgh; National Library of Wales, Aberystwyth; The Library of Trinity College, Dublin.

For me, in 1991, the magic lay in the thought that no one had touched this book in 129 years – until now.

If you're researching in a copyright library and you are presented with a book whose pages are uncut you can ask staff to cut them for you. I didn't. I had plenty of editions of Rossetti's poems in various combinations at home. I had called the book up more out of curiosity and sentiment than the need to read it. It seemed right and respectful, somehow, to allow this book to return to its dusty spot in the stacks with its virginity intact.

My motivation for doing a master's degree was rather more noble than the original reason for my first degree. In the early 1990s I had academic withdrawal symptoms. I'd enjoyed learning so much that I was hungry for more. I wanted the Open University back in my life. I now realise I should have looked around at other universities offering taught MAs by distance learning because opportunities were beginning to spring up by then. Anne Stott, my BA tutor, thought I should skip the MA stage completely and go for a DPhil – which would have meant that by now I'd be Dr Elkin, no less. I thought she had grossly overestimated my ability and didn't listen. I wish I had now because, as it turned out, an Open University MA Lit was not quite what I hoped it would be for various reasons although I ended up with more post-nominal letters (for what they're worth) and a lot of insight into a field which was more or less new to me.

At that time the Open University offered just two taught MA options in literature – the 18th century novel and 19th century poetry. I signed up for the latter. It was a two-year course so the commitment didn't feel too vast or unmanageable. By then schools were managing their own funding, rather than the money coming from Kent County Council, so it was a matter of whether or not my own school would pay for it. One of the governors interviewed me and pointed out that as soon as I'd got the qualification I'd probably move on (he was right – I did) and the school would have wasted its money. I argued that whatever happened I'd be teaching somewhere and that the wider education system would benefit. Every school hires staff who've earned their additional qualifications elsewhere so second degrees like mine were a force for the good across all schools. Extra study is never wasted. In the end I persuaded him and my MA fees were paid on the same percentage basis that they would have been if KCC had still had charge of the budget.

So I was off. Assigned to a tutor, whose name is genuinely wiped from my memory for reasons which will soon be clear, I was one of a group of five. Of these I was the only one who completed the degree. We met for occasional Saturday morning tutorials somewhere just off Finchley Road in North London where I also attended an optional weekend course, a bit like a mini-summer school. Some meetings were held in a room at London School of Economics in Holborn and on at least one occasion I went to Ms Tutor's home near Archway. Otherwise it was the usual 'course materials' at home which were nothing like as attractively presented as the BA ones I loved so much.

The first months of the course were partly devoted to research skills and, given the journalism I went on to do later, this was an indispensable eye-opener. The major first year assignment was based on combing 19th century issues of *The Athenaeum* and other publications and drawing conclusions about contemporary attitudes to poetry from reviews. And that was why I was in the British Library. I also used Senate House, the University of London library because some issues were unaccountably missing from the British Library. It was a big, time consuming – but oddly addictive – project. I would go to London from Kent for the day by train – usually in a school half term when I'd go several times in the week – arrive at British Library mid-morning and call up the volumes I wanted. The system then was that you had to fill in a slip, hand it in and wait about ninety minutes for your books to arrive at your desk. So I'd then go for an early lunch to the café over the road where, in the end, the owner got to know me. Then I'd work all afternoon in the Round Room. No doubt this is all now done digitally and much faster in the new British Library in Euston Road but I'd miss the ghosts.

At one point, tired towards the end of four-hour session poring over the small print in the British Library, I noticed a small ad for someone wanting a literary secretary and recalled seeing someone offering such services in a different publication an hour or two earlier. *That's good*, I thought, *I must connect these two*. Then I remembered that I was 'living' in the 1850s and these people would have been dead for over a century. I was learning how easy it is to become totally absorbed and sucked in. When, decades later, Hilary Mantel, author of *Wolf Hall*, said that she missed a large chunk of contemporary British life because she'd been away in Tudor England, I understood in a small way, exactly what she meant.

I noticed too that for twenty years or so, in mid-19th century England, hardly anyone reviewed any sort of poetry without mentioning Dante Gabriel Rossetti as a point of reference, comparison or contrast. Most people today are very familiar with Dante Gabriel Rossetti's sumptuous art which sells for many millions, gets lots of exhibitions and is adored by people like Andrew Lloyd Webber. The poetry is far less well known although it's admired by the *cognoscenti*. It was fascinating therefore to learn, from my own research, that in his own lifetime, Dante Gabriel Rossetti (he died in 1882) was far more known, adulated and respected as a poet than as a painter.

Towards the end of the first MA year, we met Ms Tutor and each had a short one-to-one discussion with her about dissertation topics. The dissertation would be the main activity in the second year. We had by then read, and written assignments on, quite a range of 19th century poets from John Clare to Robert Browning and from Matthew Arnold to Gerard Manley Hopkins, and immersed ourselves in that strange science known as 'poetics'. Christina

Rossetti's name was familiar from the hymn book at church in my childhood. Her poem which she simply called 'A Christmas Carol' which starts 'In the bleak midwinter', was set by Gustave Holst in 1906 and has become one of the Christmas season's most popular pieces – in churches, schools, medleys of carols and in the awful musack so beloved of 21st century shops and cafes. Harold Darke, for the record, also wrote a gorgeous setting in 1909 but that tends only to be sung by choirs.

I had now read Christina's *Goblin Market* along with lots of other poems. And yes, I think I know her well enough to call her by her given name. Anyway, we have to distinguish her from her siblings: Dante Gabriel, William Michael and Maria Francesa, all born in the late 1820s to an Italian immigrant father and a half Italian mother. Christina, who arrived in 1830, was the youngest.

I was very taken with the scampering, manic language of *Goblin Market* which is a longish narrative poem about a pair of sisters who were tempted by the fruit sold by nearby goblins. One succumbs and has to be rescued by the other. It is impossible to miss the sexual undercurrents. Well, given that Christina was a passionately pious high Anglican who turned down two possible marriages on religious grounds, I found this tension intriguing.

At that meeting I told Ms Tutor that I wanted to study Christina Rossetti and she, obviously, asked me what aspect of Rossetti's work I wanted to focus on. At that stage I had, frankly, no idea but I mentioned the erotic charge in *Goblin Market* and she pounced with glee. "That's a wonderful idea," she said, immediately coming up with a title and left me thinking that I was in a corner so I'd better just get on with it.

And that was where the rot set in. I didn't know it at the time but Ms Tutor was busy co-writing a book about penis envy and, presumably, how it is presented in literature as she was an English Literature specialist. She could think of nothing else. Every aspect of everything I wrote had to be dragged back to her pet topic.

Now, Christina was a funny old bundle of piety and passion, but I doubt very much that she'd ever seen a penis except perhaps on a classical statue and that isn't quite the same thing. When her brothers were sliding naked down the bannisters as a drunken jape with Algernon Swinburne, the poet, at Dante Gabriel's home in Cheney Walk, they didn't invite their sister round. I must have known all this at the time and why I didn't resist it, I don't know, except that I assumed this woman, with her high level qualifications, had been appointed to the Open University so surely she would have expertise and knowledge beyond mine. In the end I submitted a twenty-thousand-word dissertation which was full of this distorted nonsense. It failed.

I rang Ms Tutor in fury because she'd been encouraging through the entire drafting process and never suggested for a second that there was any kind of problem with my work. Her very unprofessional response: "Well it passed when it left me. I don't know what happened after that."

Next, still in a haze of white hot fury, I spoke to the Course Director. First – and this was unprofessional too but it made me feel much better – he assured me that Ms Tutor would never work for the Open University again, thereby effectively admitting that I'd been sold very short. Second, he assigned me to another tutor so that the dissertation could be reworked and resubmitted. This chap was a lovely man, whom I remembered from the residential weekend. I had a meeting with him in a coffee bar near Victoria Station. He advised me, among other things, to remove all mention of penis envy. He also showed me, for the first time and I don't think he was meant to, the full text of the examiner's comments. One of the comments condemned as 'risible' my perfectly accurate use of the word 'eschew' as in 'Christina Rossetti eschewed marriage'. I was mortified and livid but determined.

Within two or three weeks I had re-drafted the dissertation and sent it off – with a lot of practical support from Nick because he knew how battered I was feeling. Ten days later I got the good news that it had passed. Honour was thus saved all round although Mr Course Director told me apologetically that I would be too late to graduate that year – it was March 1993 by then. "I'm not interested in playing dressing up games with the Open University," I told him crossly and loftily. "Just send me the certificate." He chuckled hollowly and did as I asked.

Thus, in 1993, I became Susan Elkin MA Lit. I often wonder what happened to the four MA students I was grouped with at the beginning of the course. Did Ms Tutor feed them her own extremist obsessions too so that they just gave up? I have recently, out of curiosity, researched books about penis envy. It is a mindset in some young girls and women which was identified by Sigmund Freud. While quite a bit has been written about it over the years I can find nothing which remotely corresponds to the book Ms Tutor was meant to be writing so presumably she never got it published. If I were a charitable woman I might be sorry about that. But, in this case, I'm not, so good riddance.

In the end, quite a lot of useful things came out of my sorry MA experience. It had turned me into a Christina Rossetti buff (I hesitate to say 'scholar' or 'expert'). I had read every biography – about six or seven of them by 1992 – and carefully drawn comparisons. I'd even constructed charts to demonstrate where they differed. And I had immersed myself in Christina's poetry much of which is both beautiful, moving, sensual and full of colour.

There's a lot we don't know about Christina because her executor brother, William Michael, destroyed her letters and papers after her death in order permanently to safeguard her privacy. His monograph at the beginning of *The Complete Poems of Christina Rossetti*, which he published in 1911, is therefore an important source material for biographers. The uncertainty, meanwhile, leads to plenty of wild speculation. Was she abused by her father in childhood? Did she have a passion for, and relationship with, Scottish artist, William Bell Scott (1811–1890)? Was the mysterious illness she had in her teens something grimly gynaecological? It's all pretty unlikely and not supported by evidence.

What we do know is that she didn't marry James Collinson, a painter and one of the original seven pre-Raphaelites who used to meet at the Rossetti family home, because he was a Catholic. They were engaged and he converted to Anglicanism only to revert later and the engagement had to be broken off. She was, by all accounts, very distressed by this for a long time.

Later she didn't marry linguist and scholar Charles Cayley either, although they were fond friends and remained so until his death in 1883. Cayley was an atheist and, it seems, Christina couldn't countenance bringing children into a household which wasn't totally committed to Christianity.

She published several volumes of poetry the most famous of which was *Goblin Market and other poems* in 1862 for which her brother Dante Gabriel provided illustrations. Of course, during the course of my MA I collected copies of them all – many from second-hand bookshops. Today my favourite for the occasional dip is a neat slim volume from Carcanet: *Christina Rossetti Selected Poems* edited by CH Sisson (1984). My copy has on the cover what I think is the prettiest portrait of Christina ever: a chalk drawing by Dante Gabriel in 1866, she sits at a table with a book open before her, resting her face against her right palm and gazing thoughtfully into the distance. The original is in a private collection but I've seen it several times in exhibitions.

She died of breast cancer in 1894 having already survived a mastectomy which is a dreadful thought. Yes, they had anaesthetic by then, but it would have been fairly basic. In her final days she was in such agony that she had to be tied down to the bed. Why on earth didn't they give her some of the opiates which had eventually killed her drug addict brother, Dante Gabriel? I don't know the answer to that unless her religious beliefs prevented it. I, literally, shudder at the thought of such appalling suffering.

Christina has served me quite well over the years. I wrote an article for *The Independent* to mark the centenary of her death, for instance. Soon – back in English teacher mode – I wrote some A Level resources for an education publisher because some of Christina's work was on the syllabus for one of the exam boards.

Then there was the *Dictionary of National Biography*, originally edited by Virginia Woolf's father, Sir Lesley Stephen, and published in 1885. It was fully updated a century later and published in 2004 in sixty volumes and online. I was an established writer in a range of fields by then, of which more in Chapter 12, and I wrote several short biographies for the new *Dictionary of National Biography* including James Collinson, Charles Cayley and Maria Francesca Rossetti – just three of the 50,113 biographical articles therein.

Christina also led me via the pre-Raphaelites and William Morris, who was a close friend of Dante Gabriel, towards the early 20th century arts and crafts movement and furniture making. It linked with my upbringing in the antiques trade and I wrote many thousands of words on the subject.

We asked Nick's cousin, Bernard, who'd been best man at our wedding fifty years earlier, to read Christina's poem 'Remember' at Nick's funeral in 2019. It seemed appropriate because Christina, Nick and I had come quite a long way together. Although the poem has become a popular choice for funerals it still feels very fresh to me, possibly because I'm familiar with so much more of her poetry than many people.

During lockdown I did several Zoom talks for my local (Bromley) U3A group, one of which was entitled 'The life and work of Christina Rossetti'. I was then asked to do it again for a larger U3A group serving the whole of London, which was gratifying because it showed that people must have liked it the first time. The discussions at the end of the talk certainly indicated real interest both times. So no learning is ever wasted and, thirty years after I completed my MA, Christina continues to earn her keep on my bookshelves.

12. WRITING

Writers' and Artists' Yearbook (every year)

In 1957, when I was ten, I won a writing prize in a TV competition.

It was set up for Associated Rediffusion, and presented by Peter Ling and Hazel Adair, writers who went on to create *Crossroads* in 1964. They wrote an opening episode of a children's thriller and the competition brief was to write the next episode either as a synopsis or in play form. A month later the winning entry would be dramatised and broadcast so entrants had to work fast. It was ongoing for six episodes with the plot entirely in the hands of the winning children. Encouraged by my parents, I entered all six times. I was highly commended twice and was joint winner for the final episode, which won me a Parker propelling pencil that I still have. I'm afraid I remember nothing at all about the plot.

It was heady stuff, though. At that time there were only two TV channels so viewing figures were sky high. Almost every child in my school saw it, for example, and other people's parents whom I didn't know at all came over to congratulate me. My father, who was quite adept at penning things himself – witty ripostes, funny songs and the like – said: "Well that's something you could do. You could be a writer."

Me? Never! Far too much like hard work. I was going to be a teacher and had made that decision before I even started school. Nonetheless it was true that I could write. I never had any difficulty setting ideas down on paper – at school and college, in long letters to my school friend who went to live permanently in Italy when we were twenty-two (these days we email or WhatsApp), and to my mother back in London, and later Kent, while we were living in the Midlands. I also usually got the job of writing, for example, minutes of meetings or policies in teaching posts too because I didn't struggle with it as many others did. As long as I knew what I wanted to say, the words flowed pretty easily. A fellow student at Bishop Otter who'd been to some poshly expensive, but clearly useless, independent school asked me to help her with her essays because she had the thoughts but couldn't express them and I suppose that said something about me. I regarded it as nothing more than a useful skill attributable to eclectic reading.

The idea of writing more seriously must, however, have lurked in the recesses of my mind for a long time. When my father saw an offer to buy two new word processors at a discount and tentatively asked if I was interested, something snapped and I said, "Let's do it." Thus in 1989, I acquired an Amstrad 9512. I told the incredulous Nick that I was going to have a go at fiction, and I thought I was. In the event the writing took a different direction.

For years, I'd been reading columns in newspapers, noticing how they were constructed and thinking, *I could write something like that*. So one day in 1990 I did exactly that. I was, by then, Head of Upper School in a girls' high school in Kent and had set up some rather grown-up, bought-in management training for our group of twenty prefects whom we took off timetable for two days to show how important we thought the learning was. I think this is pretty standard now but it was certainly unusual, and possibly unique, when we first did it. I thought teacher readers of the *Times Educational Supplement* – still then part of *The Times* newspapers – might be interested. So I typed a piece, printed it out on my rattly old daisy wheel printer and posted it to the *Times Educational Supplement* with a covering letter.

Then I got an acceptance letter. "They'll pay you for that," said my father. Really? That had simply not occurred to me. He was right, though. In due course the piece was printed and I received a cheque for £48 which felt like a million dollars for not a lot of effort. Actually, had I but known it, the *Times Educational Supplement* had two rates: one for moonlighting teachers and the other for proper journalists. Of course they'd paid me the former but, to me, it felt like a real accolade.

Well, that was easy, I thought. *What else can I write about?*

In the early 1990s all the broadsheet newspapers devoted a whole page to education every week and it usually included an opinion piece. So for my next venture I wrote a piece about hymn signing in school assemblies. I argued with passion that traditional hymns are an essential part of our heritage and that children, of all backgrounds, should experience both the words and the melodies. I am not a religious believer, I pointed out, but believe that some things are culturally more important that any individual's doctrinal squeamishness. Moreover hymns teach vocabulary: 'slow to chide and swift to bless', 'Lo he abhors not' and 'their thirst to assuage'. Please spare us, and our children, the tinkling banalities of John Rutter and start exposing them to this time-honoured body of shared musical experience. How else will they appreciate *Abide With Me* when they hear it at the Cup Final? It was overstated and very slightly tongue-in-cheek but I had a lot of fun writing it and felt a big sense of satisfaction when it was finished.

I gulped and sent it to John Clare, education editor at *The Daily Telegraph*, thinking that my chances were minimal but that you might as well start at the top. Within a few days he wrote back, said he liked it very much and would publish it soon. For this I eventually got a fee of £175, which really was quite a lot of money in 1991. On the day that it was published I got phone calls from almost everyone I knew, lots of people at school commented and within days the *Telegraph* sent me a big packet of correspondence. And I floated about on a cloud of incredulous excitement.

So I sent John another and he took it. Then another. And suddenly I seemed to be turning myself into a writer. These early pieces often followed the same sort of pattern, I'd pick something which had disappeared from schools and argue forcibly that it should be rescued. Among many other topics I wrote about *the King James Bible*, nursery rhymes, Shakespeare, and *the Book of Common Prayer*. Nick once joked that I should compile them all into a book called *Bring Back...* Gradually I started writing more general opinion pieces too. For example, when *Middlemarch* was serialised on TV I extolled the virtues of George Eliot's masterpiece and roundly condemned the BBC 1994 version, directed by Anthony Page, arguing that it was a danger to education. By then I knew John Clare well enough to phone him and discuss the topic I had in mind rather than sending pieces in on-spec. Occasionally he'd phone me with an idea too. And after a while he took to inviting me to do the occasional feature rather than an opinion piece, which usually meant making visits or talking to people on the phone – and bit by bit I taught myself how to do out-on-the-road journalism. Working with very basic technology, I would write whatever it was in an evening, print it and then post it at the nearby central post office to catch the 11.00pm collection (yes, really). That meant that, more often than not, it was on John's desk first thing the next morning.

So what about the other broadsheets? Well I did eventually manage to get one into *The Guardian* but it was a one-off. I was more successful with *The Independent* where, with perseverance and a few false starts, I became a regular and had a bit of luck because Mary Dejevsky, comment page editor, spotted something I'd written for the education page and asked if she could have it instead. After that she frequently commissioned me to write topical comment pieces mostly on education or child-related issues. She'd ring me in the morning, talk to me about the subject they wanted explored and then I'd have to get copy to her later that day – we were using fax by then. There was one memorable week when I had a substantial piece in three different national broadsheets on different days.

The big turning point came early in 1993. I'd been applying for deputy headships because I thought it was the next logical career move. Over two years or so I was turned down for about fifty posts. Part of the problem is that forty-five was the wrong age for this. It means you probably won't move on to a headship and the school could be stuck with you for twenty years. New blood is healthy. Old blood tends to cause clots. You're supposed to be ready for deputy headship in your thirties. Moreover, I naively thought that my writing portfolio was a big USP. I suspect recruiting panels, most of them pretty insular, thought otherwise and regarded me as a potential liability.

The school I was teaching in was, by now, becoming uneasy too. Obviously I never named it in print but I wrote things which were – for some of my colleagues including the Head and governors – far too close to home.

In the February of that year I was interviewed for a deputy headship at Rochester Girls' Grammar School. It was a gruelling and very uncomfortable day. Five of us arrived at 9.00am and were still there at 7.00pm. We were required to jump through some horrible hoops including the contrived artificiality of chairing a meeting under the observation of the selection panel. The participants at the 'meeting' were the other candidates so everyone was deliberately trying to trip up everyone else. I can chair a meeting as well as anyone and have done so hundreds of times but not under those circumstances. At the end of the ten-hour day they told us that they'd decided not to appoint any of us. None of us was what they were looking for.

I drove away crying tears of frustration and relief that it was all over and asking myself why I was continuously putting myself through this misery. When I got home, Nick, who was assembling the supper that I'd put ready hours earlier, said: "There was a phone call for you. I've left the message on your dressing table." It was from John O'Leary, education editor of *The Times* to whom, for the first time, I'd sent an on-spec piece. Yes, he wanted to publish it so please would I send a photograph. I looked at this and heard a very loud voice in my head: *Forget deputy headships*, it said, *this is what you ought to be doing.*

So I went downstairs, where Nick had opened some wine, partly to cheer me up and partly to celebrate that message, and told him what I'd decided. I would resign my full-time job that summer and see if I could make it as professional writer. To ensure that we'd be able to eat I would look for a part-time post without any additional responsibilities. If I couldn't find such a job, I'd do a couple of days' supply teaching each week.

In the event, a few days later, there was a row at school about something I'd written in the *Daily Express* so I told the Head what I'd decided. I offered her my resignation, which she accepted without acrimony, although I continued to the end of the summer term. The die was therefore cast.

It was Nick who, in March, spotted an advert in the *Kent Messenger* for a part-time job in an independent school of which more in Chapter 13. He'd cut it out and left it on my desk with a note: 'What about this one?' Reader, I got the job. I never had to do any supply teaching and we always had food in the cupboard.

Meanwhile I'd bought *1993 Writers' and Artists' Yearbook* (then and annually for ever after) and was busily trying to expand my writing career in as many directions as possible. It lists every publication (and these days websites and other digital resources of course) that any writer could possibly work for along with agents, publishers and a lot of generally useful information.

There were, in the early 1990s, far more print publications than there are now, and I went right though the *Yearbook* with a pencil and post-its marking any that I thought I could have a stab at. Then I'd write to them with a CV and some 'pitches'. Yes I had to learn to talk like a journalist. In normal life we'd say 'suggestions'. I bought lots of publication too because you really do need to have a proper look at the magazine or paper before you start pitching. And, of course, the more you have already published the more seriously you are likely to be taken. It's also extraordinary how many areas you can bring education to. I usually started with education and then, with luck, could branch into other things once I was established.

For example, I offered a piece to a woodwork magazine about the importance of retaining woodwork skills in schools rather than replacing them with Design and Technology. Then I started writing about woodworking personalities for that same magazine. I would visit people in their workshops and find out what they did. I know very little about the technicalities of woodwork but am pretty good at drawing people out, thanks to all those years in teaching. Sometimes I could shift it towards antiques which was what I'd grown up with. I once, for instance, interviewed John Bly who used to be on the *Antiques Roadshow* and I wrote a piece about the clocks at Belmont, near Faversham. Sometimes it was quite literally closer to the ground. I interviewed a coppicer in a wood in Kent and visited a women's woodwork course camp in a forest in Gloucestershire. Gudrun Leitz, who was leading it, made five hundred balusters, using the traditional method with a pole lathe, for the balcony at Shakespeare's Globe and I think of her whenever I go there.

Over the next few years, I wrote regularly for four woodwork magazines including a new one which asked me to write a series about the key figures in the Arts and Crafts movement, so I found out about designer craftsmen such as Ernest Gimson and Edward Barnsley. Then a publisher in Christchurch, Dorset asked me to write a full biography of one of them, which in 1998, was my first book. Long out of print now, *Life to the Lees: biography of Arthur Romney Green* wasn't great although I had a wonderful time researching it and met lots of fascinating people. With hindsight it needed a lot more copy editing but every now and again, even now, some arts scholar contacts me for permission to quote from it which is mildly gratifying.

I approached *The Stage* in about 1994 and offered them a piece about taking school parties to the theatre. Editor Brian Attwood phoned me the next day and was very keen. It was the beginning of a twenty-two-year association with *The Stage*. I wrote opinion pieces and features for nearly every section of the paper. For many years, until 2016, I was *The Stage's* Education Editor, writing three columns a week for them at one point. I wanted to review theatre too and in time became part of *The Stage's* review team covering shows of all sorts including, some years, twenty pantomimes. By Christmas I had usually decided that I never again wanted to hear the *Ghostbusters* song or see another slosh scene but inevitably I was back there eleven months later.

Kent Life was another project. It seemed a logical thing to pursue because I lived in Kent. I profiled Kent schools which meant interesting visits. I interviewed, in their homes, Kent personalities such as TV Producer Lord (John) Brabourne and his wife, Countess Mountbatten of Burma (who made me a cup of tea in a mug), and Robin Leigh-Pemberton, Baron Kingsdown, who was Lord Lieutenant of the county. The latter afterwards escorted me back to my car and closed the driver's door for me once I was in – very courtly. I also wrote for *Kent Life* about the two long distance Kent walks which Nick and I did in sections: North Downs Way and Stour Valley Way

Vegetarianism was something else I knew about. I contacted *Here's Health* and wrote a year-long cookery/food series for them. Each month I would pick an ingredient – tofu, haricot beans, cauliflower or whatever – write an introduction and then suggest six interesting things to do with it. I managed to get variations on this idea into other health magazines too.

Because books had always been such an important part of my life I wanted to do some book reviewing too. Auberon Waugh, then editor of *Literary Review*, seemed quite impressed with my CV and I used to pop into the Beak Street office to collect a book to review or I'd sort it out with him or his deputy on the phone. I did that every month for several years. I reviewed some books for *The Independent* and *Independent on Sunday* too, starting (nervously) with Edna O'Brien's *House of Splendid Isolation* in 1994 and once or twice – but my voice clearly didn't catch on there – for the *Times Literary Supplement*. I also volunteered (no fee) to review books for the *School Librarian*: a little job I have now been doing several times a year for thirty years. I'm on my fifth editor.

The key thing was, and is, if you're freelance, to have as many outlets as possible. I was still writing for national dailies as well. By then I had added *The Sunday Times* and *Daily Mail* to the list. The *Mail* was an interesting one. The slot was called 'Education Notebook' and I wrote for it for eleven years and three different editors – not every week but often two or three weeks in succession so it was almost a regular column. Often it was the strident opinion pieces which had, by then, become my trademark but equally often it was reports of education projects, some of them very upbeat and positive. I used to tell people who criticised me for my involving myself the *Mail* that this was the only paper into which I could routinely place little good news education stories. The slot was towards the back of the paper and I sometimes wondered whether editor Paul Dacre actually read it right through to the end because my bit was certainly not right-wing hand wringing.

Once you get established in journalism the ideas tend to self-perpetuate and you get threads which keep weaving. I was once commissioned to write a piece for *Good Housekeeping* about extracurricular activities for children. One of the organisations they wanted me to include was Musicale, an independent part-time music school in Harpenden owned and run by David and Gill Johnston. Afterwards Gill Johnston kept in touch. There were four Johnston children, Rupert, Magnus, Guy and Brittany, all of them promising musicians. Gill asked me if I would write a piece about her three boys who had all been choristers at Kings Cambridge and were going back to do a fund raiser there. I sold the idea to John O'Leary at *The Times* and went off to Cambridge to meet the boys.

When I got there I was met by Magnus and Guy with their father and grandmother. Rupert, then a French horn student at Guildhall School of Music and Drama, had had a near fatal road accident the day before and was in intensive care. His mother was at his side. Of course, horrified, I said we need not proceed with the interview and that I would square it with *The Times*. But no, those two extraordinarily impressive teenagers insisted; "We're going to do this interview for Rupert. And afterwards we're going to play the concert for him too. We've rearranged the programme." I was profoundly moved and humbled. I hope I did them justice in the piece I wrote.

Rupert survived and recovered the ability to play the horn although he is severely brain damaged and now lives in an institution where he plays his horn accompanied by his pianist carer. I saw some video clips recently. Many months after the accident, Gill Johnstone invited me to their home to write about Rupert and I went with a *Times* photographer whose Porsche turned out to be a useful incentive because Rupert had great difficulty focusing. He did eventually play a few bars on the horn for us. He was then taken for a ride in the Porsche where he and the photographer bonded over cigarettes. That wasn't an education piece. *The Times* ran it as a full-page feature and I had a special message from the then editor of the paper, Peter Stothard, congratulating me and saying it was the best thing I'd ever done.

Guy Johnston, cellist, went on to win BBC Young Musician of the Year in 2000 and now has an international performing career. Magnus is a professional violinist who has just been appointed concert master at Royal Opera House as well as leading orchestras and chamber groups and often appearing on Radio 3. I am still in touch with Guy via social media and have a regular invitation to the annual chamber music festival he leads at Hatfield House in Hertfordshire. Guy is now forty-two. He was about fourteen when I first had contact with his family. Journalism can sometimes be very good at continuity and spin-offs.

For eleven years I managed to combine what was effectively a full-time, full-on career in journalism with part-time teaching. Finally, in 2004, I took the plunge. With a lot of regrets and mixed feelings I resigned my teaching job and became a full-time writer.

And suddenly, miraculously, more doors opened almost immediately. A few months before I stopped teaching I was approached by a small publisher and asked to write an English textbook for prep schools. It was published just before the end of my final term and the second book in the series was commissioned on the very day I left, which seemed like an excellent omen for my new life.

I modelled the *So You Really Want to Learn English?* series very loosely on some textbooks I'd used decades earlier. There were ten chapters or units of work, each designed to provide about three weeks' work. Each chapter had a theme such as mermaids, horses, Australia or whatever. We'd start with a prose extract, usually fiction, on the theme and then pose some open-ended comprehension questions. There would also be a factual piece and some poetry all linked to the chapter's theme. Grammar, punctuation and vocabulary work was all thematic too. And each chapter ended with a list of suggested books to read and – my favourite bit – a section called 'And it you've done all that…' It consisted of tangentially related, often whacky activity ideas to get the bright child who'd whipped through the work at top speed out of the teacher's hair. The technical name for this is 'differentiation'. A nice example of it was, in a chapter on sport, I listed football team nicknames such as Gunners (Arsenal), Cobblers (Northampton), Hornets (Watford) and asked them to research how they got these names. I got a massive kick out of the creativity of all this.

I wrote a series of three of these, of which we later did revised editions. There was also a *Year Nine Book* and a teacher's guide to it too. I also wrote, for the same publisher, various revision guides for Common Entrance and for GCSE.

At the same time I began writing English Literature Study Guides for Philip Allen Updates, in some cases with a big folder of teaching resources on the same book. I knew the people at Philip Allen Updates because I'd written a few articles for their magazine while I was still teaching. Over the years I wrote guides on *To Kill a Mockingbird* (revised three times as the syllabus changed) by Harper Lee, *Anita and Me* by Meera Syal, *Purple Hibiscus* by Chimanda Ngozo Adiche, *Never Let Me Go* by Kazuro Ishiguro and *Room With a View* by EM Forster. That involved many hours of careful reading and detailed study to such an extent that I, who can't learn anything by rote, can still quote chunks of all five novels.

In the end both these small publishers were bought by Hodder. The *So You Really Want to Learn English?* books were revised and given new titles and I wrote four workbooks on spelling and vocabulary, grammar and punctuation, writing, and reading and comprehension, new for Hodder. Most of these, along with the study guides, are still in print at the time of writing although I have to say that the royalties are not what they used to be. Both percentages and sales are lower with a big publisher.

The same thing happened with Continuum for whom I wrote several how-to books for teachers and other professionals. They were commissioned by someone I used to know on one of 'my' newspapers who had gone to work for a publishing house; another example of threads working in my favour. *Encouraging Reading* and *100 Ideas for Secondary School Assemblies* did quite well but sales dropped off when Continuum was sold to Bloomsbury.

I was recommended and referred by one of the commissioning editors at *The Independent* to another small company which produced newsletters for teachers on specific topics relating to management. I edited the professional development title for two years and launched their early years title. These were printed newsletters which went out ten times a year. They were pretty expensive to subscribers so they clearly weren't going to last into the digital age although they were crammed with information. And, as always, I found I could often make second use of contacts and stories elsewhere because of course I was still writing for as many newspapers and magazines as I could persuade to take me on. It was lucrative work while it lasted too.

I was, in short, frenetically busy and within months wondering how I'd ever found time to teach as well. Fortunately, Nick was the best PA imaginable. He organised my rail tickets, sent out invoices, dealt with the accountant (we formed Susan Elkin Ltd in 2001), proofread every word I wrote, put fuel in my car and made sure it was taxed and insured, did some of the basic research and brought me endless cups of tea. For decades, moreover, I never ironed a shirt, bought a potato or put a plate in the dishwasher. I wrote and Nick did everything else except cooking for which he had no aptitude or talent. We were very much a team.

I was so busy that it was hard to make time for some of the personal writing I had a back-of-my-mind fancy to do. I had long thought that my five years teaching in Deptford back in the late '60s and early '70s would make a good tale. I wrote *Please Miss*

We're Boys on holidays over eighteen months because that was the only time I didn't have other writing to do. I kept it on my laptop completely separate from the everyday work on my PC. I wrote the final chapter in a hotel room in Tofino on Vancouver Island in Canada in 2012 while Nick was out whale watching. We'd been out to see gorgeous bears the day before but big creatures lurking in deep water are not my thing, at all. I then self-published *Please Miss We're Boys* on Amazon and finally got it published professionally by The Book Guild in 2019.

Inevitably some of the doors have closed, or part-closed, as the years have passed. I didn't do much (although there has been a bit) for *The Daily Telegraph* after John Clare retired, for example. *The Stage* has moved on too. 'Education Notebook' was replaced by something else in *Daily Mail*. And I no longer have my PA so there's less time for writing because I have to do all the jobs, both administrative and domestic.

These days I do a lot of theatre reviewing for *Sardines* website, and occasional features for their quarterly magazine. I also write most of the copy for a bi-monthly print magazine called *Ink Pellet* which is an arts magazine for teachers so, yes, I'm still interviewing a wide variety of actors, writers, musicians and educationists and reviewing lots of books. *Musical Theatre Review* is a website for which I often review shows and I write for *Drama and Theatre*, another print magazine.

It's sad that Peter Ling died in 2006 and Hazel Adair in 2015. I really should have contacted them and thanked them because it's been quite a journey. And it's not over yet, I still pounce on *Writers' and Artists' Yearbook* and peruse it with glee, pencil in hand, each year. I'm always open to ideas and offers. Contact me if you have any.

13. A LEVEL

Cat's Eye by Margaret Atwood (1988)

So, in autumn 1993, I went to teach part-time in a boarding school in rural south Kent, driving the 25 miles across country three times a week. And it was the most stimulating, congenial, bookish teaching job I ever had. It was like stepping off an overcrowded, noisy, standing-room only, rush hour bus and climbing into a smooth, efficient, air conditioned car on a clear road. And part of that relief came from relinquishing all management responsibility. All I had to do was to turn up and teach my lessons, which any teacher knows is the best part of the job and why we go into it in the first place. My students, moreover, were almost all keen, courteous, affable and interested. How could I not be the happiest teacher in the world?

When Nick spotted the ad in the *Kent Messenger* his attention fell on it because we knew the school very slightly for two reasons. First, Lucas had attended several Kent County Council music summer schools there and we'd attended his end-of-course concerts. Second, Lucas had, at age thirteen, won a music scholarship to an independent school nearer to home. His English teacher (GCSE and A Level) was now head of department in the school I was applying to so he and I were acquainted in a small way.

I went to the interview thinking I stood no chance whatever. I hadn't been anywhere near a Russell Group university. I'd been in non-selective eleven–sixteen schools for most of my career and had never had the opportunity to teach A Level so why on earth would they want me?

I had a very pleasant chat with the Head and her deputy at the formal interview. She'd read a lot of my writing and seemed very positive about it – especially at the prospect of getting someone who actually earned half her living from professional writing to impart skills to her students. "I'm a great believer in getting people who can actually do what they're teaching," she said. I learned later that the head of Music she'd appointed was a highly experienced, charismatic practitioner but with no teaching experience at all. She certainly meant what she said.

My MA had been confirmed in the gap between my applying for the job and the interview so I was able to say nonchalantly: "Oh and by the way I now have an MA Lit in 19th century poetry. I didn't mention it on my application because with everything else I've been doing it took a bit longer to complete than it should have done." Well, it was almost the truth. It didn't seem quite the moment to discuss penis envy.

Afterwards I was shown round the school by a member of the English department and I suppose she was assessing me too. Then I had tea in the common room, sitting round in a little group with the rest of the department. By then my guard had dropped and I'd forgotten that they were trying to get the measure of me and would be sharing their views later. It felt more like sitting with colleagues. They were looking forward to an author visit event that evening with Marina Warner and mentioned, a bit anxiously *Indigo*, her latest (1992) novel which none of them had read. I had and was able to tell them that it's a reworking of *The Tempest* and does for the play rather what Jean Rhys's *Wide Sargasso Sea* does for Jane Eyre. Jaws dropped and smiles widened faces as they thanked me.

Maybe that was what swung it. The first class degree was probably a big factor. Or perhaps the head of department simply wanted someone he knew, however superficially and persuaded the Head. Either way I had a phone call the next day from the Head to offer me the post. I then had to ask about salary because, after all this was a big step for me, and money hadn't been mentioned. She said she'd consult the bursar and call me back.

"We'll match what you're getting pro rata for part-time," she said airily, an hour or two later. "Will that be OK?" Bearing in mind that, in my eleven–sixteen school in Chatham, I was on scale four, then the top level for teachers below deputy head and had maximum increments because I'd been at it for a long time, this was a remarkable offer.

"Thank you," I said, trying to sound calm and not letting my amazement and excitement show in my voice. "That's fine. Thank you. I'm happy to accept the post."

Then somehow I had to learn how to teach A Level and once I'd come down from my high I was terrified. Inevitably, when you start a job like that you are taking over from someone else and there will be exam classes who are half-way through the course. Thus I acquired a 'half cooked' A Level group, a pretty anxious GCSE group as well as groups of my own who were just starting their exam courses. When I went down for an orientation visit during the summer term I was put in with the A Level group to meet them. My instructions were to go through the possible prose texts on the syllabus with them and let them choose which one we'd do in the following term. I'd had no warning about this but fortunately I knew all the texts on the list and was eventually able to steer them towards *Hard Times*. It is, I think, a pretty silly idea to invite the students to choose because they almost certainly don't know the books. The teacher is in a far better position to do the choosing. I think I passed muster with the students on this occasion, though. They seemed friendly and positive but this was very unlike any teaching I'd done before.

I turned up in September via a welcome drinks party for new staff and their spouses, the night before term started. I met a lot of people and realised just how pleasant and warm everyone was. I made a point of attending that drinks party every year after that because I never forgot how it helped me when I was new and nervous.

The next day was devoted to induction for me and seven or eight other new members of staff, not just teachers. That was pretty terrifying too. We were warned to be very careful about mentioning the school when we were out and about. "If you have a road accident or get divorced the press will be interested in you because you work here," the Development Director told us. I wonder if her current equivalent is giving the same advice. I sat recently in a coffee shop in Ashford, and overheard a young maths teacher talking to an older woman, probably his mother, about his work and prospects at the same school. He kept mentioning the name. I had to exercise a lot of self-control to stop myself going over to him and saying "Shh. Don't they tell you about discretion in public these days?"

Several years later two girls whom I taught for A Level were killed in a road accident in Africa where they were on gap year. I had taught them both the year before. The first I knew about it was a call from my editor at *Daily Mail*. He, kind thoughtful man, phoned at 9.00pm to tell me because he knew where I taught and didn't want me to see it first in the paper. I gave him the Development Director's private phone number which was protocol because we weren't supposed to talk to the press – although my foot-in-both-camps position was, of course, pretty unusual. The next morning there was a huge photograph of one of my former students on the front page of *The Times* and I was really grateful to have been forewarned.

What I loved most about the job was sharing books with other people. As always, I devoted regular chunks of class time to talking about reading and simply sitting silently doing it, as well as teaching the examination syllabus. There wasn't much pressure to work in any particular way. Provided your students got the high level results the school expected then how you did it was more or less up to you and I liked that.

Over my eleven years in that school I taught a wide range of texts and *Cat's Eye* was one of my favourites. Margaret Atwood is a very dense, intense, intelligent writer although apart from *The Handmaid's Tale*, which is clearly a masterpiece, I prefer the non-dystopian novels.

With Atwood you have to read every word and notice what's on the page. On the face of it the writing seems very accessible but if you try to skim or stop concentrating you'll miss something important. *Cat's Eye* is a fine example of that. Elaine, the narrator, is remembering her school days and describing her friendship with two other girls one of whom, Cordelia, is a deeply troubled, complicated bully. Elaine, however, is suffering from a form of post-traumatic memory loss and denial. Then on page 398 in a 421-page novel, triggered by finding a tiny article from childhood, comes the pivotal sentence: 'I look into it, and see my life entire'. It's like a Rubiks Cube clicking into place. But if you blink you'll miss it. It was a tremendously satisfying novel to help students to unravel until, in the end, most of them loved it as much as I did. *Surfacing*, an earlier (1972) Atwood title, which I taught to one group not long before I finally left teaching, is even more opaque and really does have to be read very attentively. On a much more basic level, in both novels Atwood gives us a gloriously colourful account of camping in the remoter parts of northern Quebec. You can sense the raw reality of it so it's no surprise to learn that in childhood this is what she did with her family while her entomologist father studied forest insect life during his vacations from Toronto

University. It's yet another example of the incidental learning and vicarious experience which comes from reading fiction.

Inevitably I taught texts such as John Steinbeck's *Of Mice and Men*, JB Priestley's *An Inspector Calls*, and *Death of a Salesman* to examination groups along with masses of Shakespeare (see Chapter 4). *Major Barbara* was an interesting discovery. I'd neither read nor seen it although I remembered references to it in the Blue Door Theatre books I'd read in my early teens. Now, I studied it, taught it and enjoyed a production of it in 1999 with Peter Bowles as Undershaft and Jemma Redgrave as his daughter, the titular Barbara. As ever, I was learning alongside the students.

Poetry also featured on GCSE and A Level syllabuses, often for the former, an eclectic anthology provided by the examining board. My favourite was the selection of Keats that I taught several times to A Level students – the Open University module on the Romantic Poets that I'd done in the 1980s certainly wasn't wasted.

I tried always to stretch the students. I decided to do *Great Expectations* with one GCSE group knowing that a parallel group was doing *Roll of Thunder Hear My Cry* by Mildred D Taylor (1977). "By all means read *Roll of Thunder* independently," I told them, "it's an excellent and interesting book about the hardships of black Americans in the southern states in the 1930s. Then we could spend a lesson discussing it. But for GCSE we're going to do something more challenging that you probably wouldn't manage alone. Don't moan at me, please, when the others seem to be having it easier. In six months' time you'll thank me." I was right. They did.

I wasn't always successful, though. One year I picked *Barchester Towers* from the A Level set books list. I've loved it for decades and I've always thought it was one of the funniest books in English so I was confident I could carry the students along with me. Rarely have I got it so wrong. They loathed it and it wasn't long before I was bitterly regretting my choice but we were too far in for a U-turn by then. Most of them knew nothing about church history and didn't want to know either. I, of course, had grown up attending an Anglican church which was virtually Anglo-Catholic. I'd followed Christina Rossetti's religious struggles and I'd read some of John Henry Newman's poetry for my MA as well as knowing and loving Elgar's *The Dream of Gerontius*. I understood the issues. I simply couldn't make the students see that mid 19th century church politics and the dichotomy between the low and high church factions is not only interesting but vital to an understanding of Trollope's humour and the events in *Barchester Towers*. They all passed A Level with good grades but only because they were hard working and conscientious. Wherever those girls, women long since, are now I expect they still shudder when they remember *Barchester Towers* and I bet none of them went on to read the other five novels in the series, which is a pity. And it was all my fault.

For many years I bought all the novels on the Booker Prize shortlist which I would then read before the announcement of the winner. It was partly a way of forcing myself to keep up to date with new writing and exploring authors I might not otherwise have discovered. It was why, for instance, I'd read Salman Rushdie's *The Satanic Verses* in 1988 several months before Ayatollah Khomeini, supreme head of Iran, got wind of it, had copies burned and declare a fatwah, or death sentence, on Rushdie at which point the book became headline news – and sales rocketed. I talked to the girls all the time about my discoveries and shared thoughts. I always placed my current book on the desk when I unpacked my bag at the beginning of each lesson and it was often an informal talking point as they arrived or left.

Sharing books didn't stop in the classroom either. For the first time I was working closely with people who were passionate about books although tastes varied, obviously. English department chat in breaks almost always came back to books and reading. It didn't end there. I have recently spent time with one of my former colleagues, twice at her home in Cornwall and once at mine in London. We've always kept distantly in touch but since lockdown have now rekindled a proper friendship. She's terrific company and we have lots in common. Her bookshelves are a joy to browse and I reckon we talk about books for at least half of the time we're together. I'm forever pulling out my phone and noting or ordering titles she has mentioned and sometimes it feels, delightfully, like being back in the common room.

That addictive bookish camaraderie went beyond the English department too. A colleague in the history department, who went on to write two books of her own, would often sit with me and sometimes some of the others. She was very widely read and we'd swap book titles. I met her for lunch a couple of times after we had both left the school. Sadly, she died while still only in her early sixties. I attended her memorial service in Tudley Church, near Tonbridge, which is famous for its Chagall stained glass and where my colleague had been a volunteer guide. I sat gazing at them and thought about all the books she and I had shared so happily.

Fitting in the two parallel jobs was as liberating as I'd hoped. For the first time I had term time days when I didn't have to be in a classroom. I used to joke that it took me until I was forty-six to leave school – and even then only partly. I quickly realised that if I taught Saturday mornings I'd only need to do two weekdays which gave me an extra day for journalism. Most teachers, apart from the ones who lived on site, detested Saturday mornings, so my volunteering for it went down well and saved someone else from having to do it.

The students were fascinated by my dual role. Most of the nationals were delivered to the boarding houses in an effort to encourage students to develop a newspaper habit. It meant they saw a lot of what I wrote and would often want to discuss the issues, sometimes challengingly (but never rudely), which was healthy. And I wrote better, especially about education, because I was in regular contact with young people. I wasn't just a journalist observing from outside. It got me a lot of respect from parents as well because they too saw a lot of what I wrote.

I took great care not to bite the hand which was feeding me by implicating the school in my writing but I did, once or twice, sail close to the wind and resort to a pseudonym. A change of sex is an effective disguise so I usually picked a male name. Once I wrote a scurrilous, damning – but completely honest – account of GCSE. If anyone at school had known it was me there would have been real trouble. I'm sure they had their suspicions but there was no way they could prove it. Dear John Clare at *The Telegraph* channelled my payment though his own personal bank account to secure my anonymity and ensure that no one at the paper, in the accounts department for example, would be able to connect it with me and leak it.

It was a bit odd when, as a journalist, I visited other schools of which I was now free to do a lot more. I spent a night with the monks, teachers and students at Ampleforth for a piece in *The Times*, for instance. In relation to various projects I visited, among many others, Tonbridge School, Haileybury, Kings Canterbury, prep schools all over the country and lots of state schools. On one occasion I went to visit an innovative primary school in Orkney for *The Times*. A flight from Gatwick to Inverness, a much smaller one to Kirkwall and a quasi-minibus with wings to Sanday and back the same way the next day. I usually kept quiet about my teaching and where I did it when I was in another school in a totally different capacity but at Ampleforth, when I found myself being shown round by the brother of one of my A Level students, of course he knew exactly who I was.

Somehow I juggled the time. When I went on a four-day press trip to Egypt (Luxor, Cairo and Sharm El-Sheikh) in 2002 with six other journalists and a commission from *Best* magazine, we had a couple of hours 'free' on the last afternoon. I sat outside my

Sharm room in the sunshine and marked a pile of *Henry V* essays.

I was a useful staff member too. Sometimes my own school would court me to write about projects and I did my best to place such stories, sometimes successfully. Freelance journalists, though, can only ever get something published if they can persuade an editor to run with it. And no editor wants anything which smacks of promotion. Ironically I have, in the year of writing, for the first time helped the school with its alumni magazine for which I have written two articles and done a fair amount of commissioning and editing: another circle completed.

14. ALZHEIMER'S

Elegy to Iris by John Bayley (1998)

For anyone remotely interested in books and literature, writer John Bayley's tender account of his wife, Iris Murdoch's, work, life, illness and death was irresistible. She was, after all, in her fiercely cerebral way, one of the biggest names and most respected authors of the second half of the 20th century. So, I read it.

It's a moving love story – effectively an account of their life together from first meeting – as well as detailing her final, tragic trajectory into Alzheimer's. Like many people I've met since, I hadn't, before Bayley's book, understood that Alzheimer's is a progressive, terminal disease of the brain. It therefore gradually, or sometimes rapidly, affects and knocks out all body functions until the body dies. Alzheimer's disease is a great deal more than forgetfulness. And it's nonsense to say nobody dies from it. They do. All the time. Iris Murdoch had no other illness any more than Nick did.

In 2002 it was released as an outstanding film, directed by Richard Eyre, simply entitled *Iris*, with Jim Broadbent as Bayley, Judi Dench as Murdoch and Kate Winslett as Murdoch's younger self. Unusually, I saw it alone at the cinema in Sittingbourne because Nick had broken several bones in his foot a week before and, about to have reconstruction surgery, was more or less immobile. As things turned out I was later quite glad that he didn't see it because the film is a stylishly graphic revelation of what Alzheimer's does to you and he might have remembered it when he was facing his own diagnosis.

Nick had always been mildly eccentric. He was elaborately picky about food, with a list of dislikes so long and complicated that invitations to other people's homes were often an embarrassment. He insisted on rolling his socks in a particular way and lining them up in the drawer in colour order. He would cross the road to avoid walking past a garden with a tall sunflower towering above him ("remind me of Triffids and I don't like their faces") and refused to eat off one of our Portmeirion tea plates because the Colchium (meadow saffron) design looked like a star fish. He wasn't great at small talk and could be awkward in company.

He mellowed somewhat over the years, and became more confident, but generally I accepted his personality quirks because it was 'my normal'. I suspect that now he'd probably be diagnosed as being on the autistic spectrum, at the very mild end. Either way it meant that when Alzheimer's crept into our lives, it was a long time before I recognised that there really was something wrong. It seemed like Nick just being Nick. Looking back now I can see that it was staring me in the face but I didn't spot it.

From at least the millennium year I would often tell him something such as "Felix will be here at about 5.00pm."

Next thing I knew he'd say: "Felix is outside parking. Were we expecting him?"

Then I'd respond, "Yes, I told you this morning," which would trigger a pointless no-you-didn't / yes-I-did conversation until, weary with frustration, I'd get cross and stomp off – to make a cup of tea for Felix in that instance. It was infuriating but I thought it was just a Nick-ism, and that like many a husband before and since, he was not listening to his wife. I just got into the habit of writing important things down or making sure that he did.

On one occasion, a friend was present, at one of these heated interchanges so I turned to her and said: "I really did say it, didn't I?"

She responded quietly: "Yes, you did. I heard you." It made me feel better but it didn't occur to me that we were lurching into Murdoch/Bayley territory. It should have done.

Meanwhile Nick had long since lost his sense of smell. We'd laughed about the oddness of that and agreed that it was probably better than losing sight or hearing in your fifties. Lucas cheerfully put in extra smoke alarms, joking that: "You're a liability and not fit to be left in the house on your own since you can't smell burning." Taste had almost gone too, which meant that he was gradually becoming easier to feed. I don't think it would have helped any of us to know that anosmia, loss of a sense of smell, is a well-documented and very common precursor of Alzheimer's.

Another odd thing was that he had suffered from urinary urgency for decades. I lost count of the number of times I pressurised him into having his prostate checked but the result was always normal. Doctors valiantly made other low-key suggestions, but no one came up with a helpful explanation. Meanwhile his worsening need to stop at far more motorway service stations, public loos and bushes than other people was at best tiresome and, at worst, seriously inconvenient. Sometimes I'd get irritated and snap: "Oh for goodness' sake! Most men your age have an enlarged prostate and it's fixable. Why on earth do you have to get some other weird, undiagnosable thing?" I realise now that it was almost certainly Alzheimer's taking little nips at the bladder-control bit of the brain and wish that I hadn't been quite so bad tempered about it because the constant fear of accidents was pretty stressful for him.

Then there was sense of direction. If we were walking in an unfamiliar town, by about 2010, he'd become very vague about finding his way back to the car and apparently had no sense of where things were in relation to anything else. He also got nervous about parking in tight spaces and usually asked me to do it.

I finally joined the dots and realised that there really was something wrong early in 2016 when he started sending incorrect invoices to my clients. This was totally unheard of for my meticulous, efficient Nick and I was horrified. I sorted it with the clients, fortunately all people I knew quite well, and told Nick to leave invoicing to me from there on.

I also told him that I thought we should seek medical help for his memory problems (and, as usual, the urinary ones) as soon as we'd accomplished the big house move from Kent to London which finally happened in September 2016. He agreed meekly. He knew as well as I did that there was something seriously wrong – especially as he managed to lock himself out of the house early in the week of our move. I was working in central London and I had to tell him to come up to town from Sittingbourne and get keys from me. He got lost – because he couldn't remember the name of the theatre I was in. "Worst day of my life," he said afterwards in acute distress. Yes, the signs were there, all right.

I've written extensively elsewhere about Nick's illness (*The Alzheimer's Diaries*, The Book Guild, 2022) so don't propose to detail it again here. Suffice it to say that he was eventually diagnosed in April 2017, went downhill at breakneck speed and died in Lewisham Hospital in August 2019.

John Bayley accompanied me throughout the twenty-eight months that I was, perforce, a carer on an unsought-for downhill journey. I often thought, for example, of Bayley's comment about his lifelong fascination with the female body and now here he is hosing one down in the shower. Yes, I did a great deal of hosing down the body which I had once found exciting but which was now just a leaky, messy nuisance – while its owner stood there impassive, bemused, compliant, wet and helpless. I also watched a long, slow, inexorable end-of-life coma at the last, exactly as Bayley describes and Dench does so perfectly in the film.

I read other books about Alzheimer's during that time if they caught my eye and I'd already read and admired Emma Healey's moving novel, inspired by her grandmother, *Elizabeth Is Missing* (2015) the year before our problems became serious. On the whole, though, I read for escapism during that difficult period. I needed a respite from my worsening, day-to-day issues and, as ever, I found it in books. I could, for instance, often be found hunched at the side of his bed reading a detective novel on my iPad while Nick slumbered on during his final seven-week hospital stay.

Nick, meanwhile, had gone on reading or – I suspect – latterly, pretending to. When his job relocated in the early 1970s, he commuted to Luton first from Forest Hill and later from Wellingborough and often travelled elsewhere for work – always with a book in his hand. In the late 1980s he worked for several years as Education Officer for the Institute of Administrative Management and yes, I know it sounds like a satire but was actually a respectable and respected exam-setting body based, at that time, in Petts Wood. That took him even further afield including on one occasion to Malaysia, Singapore and Hong Kong. That twenty-three-day absence, incidentally, was the longest we were apart in our entire marriage.

It was mostly novels that he carried and read. He was, for example, tremendously taken with Philip Pullman's *Northern Lights* (1995) and the rest of the 'His Dark Materials' trilogy. I read it and thought it was admirable but it's fantasy and that has never worked for me as well as it seems to for many other people. He had a mild passion for French literature (I blame A Level French) and loved *L'Etranger* by Albert Camus.

Even before we were married he'd got immersed in Wagner's *Ring* and bought the complete set of Karajan recordings on LPs in boxes. They stayed with us right through our half century together even though in later years he had no turntable to play them on;

Lucas has them now. He found his way, via that music into Norse mythology and owned and read books about it. None of this was shared with, or by, me. I can cope with Wagner only in bite-sized chunks.

Like me he would often pull something familiar off the shelf and re-read it. He would also read anything I'd recently found and got excited about – most of my Open University set books, for example and all those Booker winners or runners up.

He had gaps, though. When we saw David Lean's wonderful film *A Passage to India* in 1984 I said something about the book and was amazed to find he'd never read it. How could any literate, educated reader have reached the age of thirty-nine and missed *A Passage to India*? I put a copy in his hand and I don't think he was disappointed.

He'd always been a newspaper reader too. We had print copies delivered, years ago by a delivery boy from a local newsagent and more recently by a company. We always had *The Daily Telegraph* because it had been the go-to paper for the previous two generations in both our families. *The Times* was our second newspaper – for balance. And when I was writing a lot for the nationals we also had *Daily Mail* on Tuesdays, *The Independent* on Thursdays and *The Guardian* on Fridays so that we saw everyone's education coverage. Nick assiduously read them all.

Then from about 2017 his reading began to slow. He'd still carry a book or, by then, often his Kindle, round the house but I noticed two things. First, if it was a hard copy he seemed to have the same book in his hand for weeks. It reminded me of students, reluctant readers, who would bring the same book to independent reading sessions all term until in the end I'd say: "You're obviously not enjoying that book. Abandon it and let's find you something you'll enjoy." But of course, Nick's problem was different. He'd fall asleep at any time of day within just a few moments of settling down with his book so there was no progress or continuity.

Second, if he was reading on Kindle I'd say casually "What are you reading?" and he could never tell me. Fair enough because I often forget titles too if I'm reading digitally and can't see the cover. So I'd ask him what it was about but he could never tell me that either.

The truth, of course, is that if you can't remember what was on the previous page, reading becomes pointless. Watching him read less and less was, for me – who can't imagine life without books – one of the saddest parts of his illness.

In his final few months he lost his literacy almost completely and that's not a symptom of end-stage Alzheimer's which gets talked about much. I'd find funny little scribblings on bits of paper where he'd tried to note something and clearly couldn't – just wobbly odd letters and the occasional nonsense word derived from a real one, like a line from James Joyce's *Finnegan's Wake*. It was another form of struggling to communicate.

The last photograph I have of Nick at home was taken on the 2nd of July 2019 when he wasn't feeling very well – he was admitted to hospital the following morning. He is sitting at the dining table with that day's *Telegraph* open on the table, still doggedly following the habits of a lifetime despite the all-embracing mental fog and the wobbly, physical malaise. Dave our big, old tabby cat has jumped onto the table and settled on the newspaper as close to Nick as he can get. Cats are good at sensing illness. Nick has nodded off with chin on chest, and is oblivious to the newspaper, the cat and me with the camera.

Alzheimer's and its effects, however, come and go randomly. It's like an old-fashioned radio, badly out of tune. If you twiddle the knob for long enough, you might catch a snatch of a radio station before it wanders off again. A week or two before Nick died, Felix – whose wife and daughters are all redheads – was standing at the foot of his father's hospital bed wearing a T shirt bearing the legend: 'A ginge is not just for Christmas'. Someone pointed it out to Nick and asked him what it said. He read it aloud effortlessly, although the joke passed him by. Reading those seven words was a long way, though, from *War and Peace* and *Les Miserables* both of which he devoured happily in the 1980s. He was streets ahead of me in some ways. I have never read either of them.

15. TODAY

Miss Benson's Beetle by Rachel Joyce (2020)

'Words, words, words' is Hamlet's rude reply to Polonius who cautiously asks what he's reading. It's a neat summary of my life so far. It's all been about words: the ones I've read, the ones I've written and the ones I've helped other people to understand.

Since August 2019 I have lived alone, for the first time in my life. I thought it would be difficult. In fact I've settled into it much more readily than I thought I would. I don't mind sleeping in an otherwise empty house – although I'm very glad that it's a small, south London semi rather than a drafty great barn in Sittingbourne. I am not fazed by coming home to it alone at night and I quite like being able to do everything my own way. For example, I now have both a blackout blind and blackout curtains in my bedroom so it really is dark which Nick, who liked light even at night, would not have agreed to.

I work most days in my upstairs office, having converted Nick's downstairs one into a music room. I am sustained by Radio 3 and, of course, by reading. Living alone, moreover, has meant that I read even more. Weak teeth force me to eat very slowly so, if I'm alone,

I read at the same time with my iPad on a stand. I also do this in cafes, restaurants and coffee shops, places which I frequent before and between work commitments, especially shows and concerts. I probably read for at least two hours a day at meal times, starting with *The Times* and *The Daily Telegraph* at breakfast. I cancelled the print subscriptions and deliveries after Nick's death and now read them the 21st century, digital way.

Then there's always a print book as well. I'm not a particularly good sleeper and all the experts counsel against screens in the bedroom so I try to stick to a 'proper' book at bedtime. But because reading is, as I was wont to tell students continually, too important to use as a mere soporific, I read my print book at other times too so that I get through it at a reasonable speed. At the time of drafting this paragraph I am deep in a re-read of *Cat's Eye* by Margaret Atwood in hard copy and Laura Shepherd-Robinson's historical thriller *The Square of Sevens* on my iPad via Kindle.

The best book I have read in the last four years was definitely *Miss Benson's Beetle*. It's a quest story, in the tradition of *The Odyssey*, *Pilgrim's Progress* and *The Wizard of Oz*, with a very unlikely protagonist. An untravelled frumpy schoolteacher, not very good at her job, inherits money and decides to journey to the other side of the world in search of a rare golden beetle that she remembers from a book of her father's. The companion she recruits to take with her is totally unsuitable but what emerges is a warmly uplifting celebration of female friendship. If you read only one of the many books I've mentioned in this book please make it this one. I don't think you'll be disappointed.

Bereavement and my new way of life were ticking along reasonably with lots of books and a busy work schedule to sustain me. Only six months later came lockdown. And that really did hurt. Not only had I lost my spouse but I couldn't see my family and work dried up overnight. It felt as if I'd lost everything and I was deeply afraid that, given my age, I would never work again.

Obviously there were plenty of people much worse off than me. I had a comfortable home, a nice park nearby to walk round and enough money to buy what I needed. Nonetheless, March 2020 felt like a pretty hideous double whammy and I was very miserable.

Naturally, I read more and more as it was about the only thing available to keep me sane. Soon I was averaging ten books a month although obviously that depends how long the books are. *Middlemarch* and *Anna Karenina*, both of which I re-read during lockdown, are much bigger reads than, say, John Steinbeck's *The Red Pony*, an old favourite to which I also returned at that time.

One day I was chatting to Karen, mother of my third granddaughter and Felix's ex. I call her my daughter-out-law and happily we're all still good friends, kinswomen as it were, in an amicable extended family. She was one of the many people who kindly made a point of keeping in regular contact with me during those bleak, lonely lockdown months. "You're always telling us about all these books you read. Why don't you start a books blog?" she said, trying valiantly to think of a constructive work activity I might occupy myself with until the powers that be allowed me out of domestic imprisonment to do some real work.

Genius! I started Susan's Bookshelves on my website (www.susanelkin.co.uk) that week with my thoughts about John Christopher's *Death of Grass* which I had just finished re-reading. The blog is, at the time of writing, well into its third year and, so far, I've written about 130 posts each on a different title. I try to keep it as broad as I can so we range over new titles, information books, biography, memoir, classic novels, poetry and anything else which takes my fancy. From time to time, I wonder whether it has run its course but I seem to have built a fan base who all tell me to carry on. So I do, although most of my 'proper' work has, thank goodness, slotted back into place as the pandemic has receded. One of my greatest fans is Karen who tells me that, thanks to me, she has 'got back into reading' and that's one of the most pleasing things about it. At heart, I'm still a teacher, desperately wanting everyone to experience total literary immersion.

The idea for this book grew from Susan's Bookshelves. I still, somehow, gobble up about ten books most months. Despite pressures of work there still seems to be time on trains, buses, at meal times and if I'm really well organised an odd half hour in the garden or sitting room with a book.

During lockdown I got into the habit, for the first time ever, of regularly watching a bit of TV in the evenings. I'd pick something, usually crime drama, and follow it through episodically over several days like reading a book. I caught up on some of the things I'd heard of over the years but never seen like *Broadchurch*, *Last Tango in Halifax* and *Unforgotten*. And yes, *Happy Valley* was brilliant. It made something to look forward to towards the end of each day and helped to shape a routine. Now that I'm back to normal, frequently out reviewing shows and concerts in the evenings, there's much less time for TV. Moreover, in recent months I've noticed that I'm slipping back to type. If I'm having an evening in I read my book over supper as usual and more often then not get so engrossed so that I'm still sitting there at 10.00pm. It's nearly bedtime and I haven't been near the television. In short, books are winning again as they always did.

So how do I choose what to read? I see reviews in newspapers or I see books mentioned on platforms such as Twitter and they grab my attention. One surprisingly good source of interesting books to read is *Good Housekeeping* (I get it free as a perk with one of my bank accounts). Quite often there is nothing to interest me in the feature pages or the cookery ones but there almost always is on the books page. *The Garnett Girls* by Georgina Moore and *We All Want to Do Impossible Things* by Catherine Newman are both examples of books I've enjoyed recently that I discovered courtesy of *Good Housekeeping*.

If I've read and liked one title by an author than I might go back and read his or her backlist and/or pre-order the next one. I've worked my way through most of Lianne Moriarty and Jane Harper on this basis, just as I did years ago with Daphne du Maurier and later with Anita Brookner.

Crime fiction has long been my go-to place for writing which manages to be both high quality but relatively undemanding. Years ago I lapped up both Ruth Rendell and PD James. These days I always pre-order Peter James. One of the things I really like about crime fiction is the way it has evolved in recent years as writers invent ever more interesting protagonists. Richard Coles's Canon Clement is, for instance, a pretty unusual sleuth and I have a lot of time for Val McDermid's Karen Pirie although less so on TV. The most original detective I've found lately is Simon Mason's DI Wilkins. He works in Oxford but, with his deprived background, scruffy clothes and off-hand manner he's about as different from Colin Dexter's Inspector Morse as could be. Another thing I warm to in these series is the overarching human story which continues from book to book, independent of the cases being solved. I'm still, at one level, the child who loved following the Famous Five as they progress, although Julian, Dick, George, Anne and Timmy don't seem to have birthdays or get any older.

I often interview writers so of course I make sure I've read some of their books because it would be, in my view, a dreadful discourtesy not to. Thus, when I met Elly Griffiths (whose real name is Domenica da Rosa) in a café in Brighton, I was able to discuss her wonderful Ruth Galloway novels with her because I'd read every single one. At her recommendation I also read some of her friend William Shaw's novels (DS Alexandra Cupidi – set in Kent – super) and later interviewed him. Not that it's always crime I read; Ellen Alpsten's *The Tsarina's Daughter*, is an engaging historical novel, set in pre-Soviet Russia and I interviewed her in a coffee bar at Tate Modern.

15. Today

Sometimes it's sheer serendipity. Felix runs a plumbing business in Brighton and found himself working in the home of writer Alison MacLeod. He asked her about her work and she told him that her latest novel *Tenderness* is about DH Lawrence. He told her about his mother and what she does. I had just re-read *Lady Chatterley's Lover* and he knew that. She kindly presented him with a signed copy of her book for me, which he gave me as part of my Christmas present in 2021. It's a really fine and original novel leading up to the 1960 trial which of course I remember clearly although I was too young to understand the real issues. Alison's very enjoyable, thoughtful novel could well have passed me by had she not hired Felix to install her new boiler.

And one thing often leads to, or hooks up with, another. An actor I admire (and have interviewed), Mark Farrelly, has a repertoire of four one-man shows. I'd seen them all except *The Silence of Snow* which is about Patrick Hamilton. When I was finally booked in to review a performance of it at Bridge House Theatre Penge, I thought it would be sensible to acquaint myself with one of Hamilton's books first so I read *Hangover Square*. Then a woman I chat to at Brighton Dome, because she sits behind when I review Brighton Philharmonic concerts, told me that she was running a study day based on Patrick Hamilton's novel *The West Pier*. So I read it and attended the study day. Meanwhile, by another coincidence, I'd reviewed *Rope*, a play by Patrick Hamilton at Upstairs at the Gatehouse in Highgate. Suddenly Hamilton seemed to be everywhere.

During and since lockdown I've done a lot of re-reading. Maybe it's something to do with age but I often think of a book I've really liked in the past and feel the urge to re-read it. It's interesting, for instance, to return to titles I used to teach to see how well I remember them. Or, often, it's simply a book I've read and been moved by in the past. Usually I'm entranced and, of course, if you go back to a novel like *Jane Eyre* as I did recently you see things in it you've never noticed before. It's almost the ultimate indicator of a really great work. All the Beethoven symphonies offer something new every time, for example.

It doesn't always work though. I read AS Byatt's *Possession* in the spring of 1990 and was bowled over. I said immediately that it would win that year's Booker prize and it did. It's a historical flashback which investigates the nature of research and proposes a relationship between two 19th century poets who bear a striking resemblance to Christina Rossetti and Robert Browning. I was so taken with it that I read it again a year later. I returned to it earlier this year and found it turgid and not very gripping. I read perhaps a quarter of it and put it back on the shelf. So something has changed in thirty-three years. It could be me. Perhaps some fiction just feels dated. And yet, when I re-read John Fowles's *A French Lieutenant's Woman* (1969) a few months ago I found it as arresting as ever.

Biography and autobiography feature quite often too. Lucas, who had that evening conducted a production of *The Sorcerer*, and I were recently discussing George Grossmith. He sang roles such as The Lord Chancellor, KoKo and John Wellington Wells in the original productions of Gilbert and Sullivan's *Iolanthe*, *The Mikado* and *The Sorcerer* among other operas. He made them his own to such an extent that they're known as the Grossmith roles. He also wrote, with his brother Weedon, the Victorian comic novel *A Diary of a Nobody*. Beyond that neither Lucas nor I knew anything about him. I said that someone must surely have written a biography and reached for my phone. I was right. Someone had although it was long since out of print. I found and ordered a second-hand copy of Tony Joseph's *George Grossmith* (1980) while still sitting in Lucas's kitchen. I have since read it with great interest and passed it on to Lucas. Grossmith, I now know, was with the D'Oyly Carte Opera Company for only seven years but had a very successful career with one man shows both in Britain and America.

15. Today

I'm regularly sent books to review for work so I often find myself studying how-to books for actors, directors or drama teachers along with young adult fiction. Both lead to doors opening because I sometimes then interview the authors. I had a good chat recently, for example, to Louisa Reid after reading her powerful verse novel *Activist* (2022) which really made me think long and hard about the way in which teenage girls are still routinely harassed and abused by boys in school while staff condone it though taking no action.

I read poetry too. As an English teacher, naturally I taught a lot of poetry over the years and it's under my skin. I often go back to re-read old favourites such as a Keats ode or almost anything by Christina Rossetti or Gerard Manley Hopkins. When Nick was dying I had an almost surreal sense that there was a poem eagerly trying to burst out of me, which is odd because I really am not a poet. I suppose it was a case of feelings so overpowering that they couldn't be expressed in any other way. So I wrote 'Letting Go' and included it in *The Alzheimer's Diaries*. Whenever I do a book talk and read it aloud now there is a very loud silence at the end and usually someone in tears, so I suppose it's quite strong. I was pleased with it, anyway. When Lucas first read it he said, "It reads like the work of someone who has read an awful lot of poetry," and that's a pretty apt description. I have.

Charles Causley (1917–2003) has always been a favourite poet and I've argued for years that he was, and is, seriously underrated. Read for example 'Death of an Aircraft' or 'Cowboy's Song' and admire his musical way with rhyme and rhythm. I was delighted, therefore, to spot and read Patrick Gale's novel about Causley *Mother's Boy* (2023) which seems to be doing well. And as a stepping stone on my reading journey it's another example of links and connections.

We all read at different levels, though, or should do. No one can read Gibbon or Tolstoy to the exclusion of all else, good and interesting as they both are. I used to tell my students this and never used dismissive terms such as 'trash', 'pulp fiction' or 'chicklit' when discussing reading. For myself I enjoy the occasional dive into, say, Katie Foorde who writes a good, honest, modern romance such as *One Enchanted Evening* (2023), or Ruth Jones whose novel *Us Three* (2020) is a good one and really entertaining. But I might be reading Dickens or Norman Lebrecht on Beethoven the week before or after or even at the same time. I get very irritated with teachers – some of my former colleagues amongst them, unfortunately – who try to tell young people what they 'should' be reading. Just keep it eclectic and do lots of it.

On the 28th of June 2023, just as I was nearing the end of writing this book, I spotted a report in *The Daily Telegraph*. A University of Cambridge study, published in the journal *Psychological Medicine*, had found the children who read for twelve hours a week do better in school than those who don't. Well to me this is blindingly obvious but as it clearly isn't to everyone I was delighted to see research to support it. Professor Barbara Sahakian, co-lead author of the study wrote: 'Reading isn't just a pleasurable experience. It's widely accepted that it inspires thinking and creativity.' She goes on to say that it improves cognition, mental health and brain structure. Yes, of course. Please tell the Government and the people who devise curricula that reading is not just about getting the decoding skills right so that you can read an engineering manual or a chemistry textbook.

When we were clearing my mother's house after her death in 2001, we found her book by her bedside with her bookmark in. It was a Minette Walters crime thriller which I had lent her. She had clearly been reading it the night before the stroke which hospitalised her and led to her death. I was moved to think that she'd been able to continue reading for pleasure, interest and entertainment to the last.

15. Today

I rather hope I die – but not just yet – with a book in my hand, and the usual TBR (To Be Read) pile nearby, so that they can say at my funeral: "She died as she lived: books, books and more books."

For writing and publishing news, or recommendations of new titles to read, sign up to the Book Guild newsletter:

SCAN ME